Books by Norma Johnston

The Keeping Days
Glory in the Flower
The Sanctuary Tree
A Mustard Seed of Magic
Of Time and Of Seasons
A Striving After Wind
The Swallow's Song
If You Love Me, Let Me Go
The Crucible Year
Strangers Dark and Gold
Pride of Lions

PRIDE
OF
LIONS

PRIDE OF LIONS

*The Story of
the House of Atreus*

Norma Johnston

ATHENEUM NEW YORK 1979

LIBRARY OF CONGRESS CATALOGING IN PUBLICATION DATA

Johnston, Norma.   Pride of lions.

SUMMARY: Retells the story of the House of Atreus
and the pride, deception, hatred, and revenge that involves
Agamemnon, Clytemnestra, and their children Iphigenia,
Electra, and Orestes.
    1. Agamemnon (Greek mythology)   [1. Agamemnon
(Greek mythology)   2. Mythology, Greek]   I. Title.
PZ8.1.J64Pr   292'.2'11   79-12463
ISBN 0-689-30711-X

Published simultaneously in Canada
    by McClelland & Stewart, Ltd.
Manufactured by Fairfield Graphics, Fairfield, Pennsylvania
Designed by Mary M. Ahern
First Edition

CONTENTS

THE
BEGINNINGS

I

THE
BEGINNING

I · THE BEGINNINGS

IN THOSE DAYS there were giants in the earth. Men and women whose pride and passions towered so they shook the world. From their citadels on the mountaintops they looked out across plains rioting with olives and with grapes to encircling mountains and the wine-dark sea. The sands and the stones they trod glittered like white gold, and the air itself danced and dazzled, and it almost seemed they could stretch out their arms and split the sky.

They called themselves the children of the gods.

This is the story of the House of Atreus, the royal race of Mycenae of the Lion Gate.

IN THE BEGINNING there was Chaos, swirling potential waiting to take form. And Chaos separated into two entities: Uranus, the male principle, the sky; Gaea, the female principle, mother earth. And Uranus and Gaea united into one harmonious and pulsing whole, and Gaea travailed in her depths and brought forth living forces.

These were the powers to which the earth gave form: Hecatonchires, of a hundred hands and fifty heads, monstrously huge

3

and strong. Cyclopes, the wheel-eyed ones, who towered like the mountain crags and were devastating, irresistible in force. And Titans, twelve in number, six male, six female, like men but far more beautiful and far more grand. These latter were the Elder Gods, the forces human instinct recognized as divine. Toward the Titans, Uranus was ambivalent; but he loathed and feared his monstrous progeny and imprisoned them in the deep darkness of the earth.

The Titan Cronos (*Time*) rose up against his father, overthrew him and mutilated him, rendering him impotent. The blood of Uranus, falling upon the earth, caused Gaea to conceive the Furies, dark hags to haunt the guilty and avenge iniquity, dwelling in the Unknown Dark.

Cronos now was lord of the universe, and he united with his sister-wife Rhea, the mother goddess, and she brought forth children. Each in turn Cronos swallowed, for he recalled how he had overthrown his father and he feared the same fate would be his in turn. But the sixth child, Zeus, Rhea brought forth in secret, and in secret he was reared to adulthood, hating and envying his father.

When he was grown, and his power was confirmed, Zeus, with Rhea's aid, forced Cronos to disgorge the children he had swallowed. Zeus called these brothers and sisters to rise against their father, and there was a great struggle in earth and heaven between the Titans, those instinctual forces, and their offspring the Olympians, the attributes of reason. Zeus also released the monstrous powers that Uranus had buried in the earth, and they fought on the Olympians' side. For age upon age the battle raged, and the earth shook with the tread of the divine warriors, and the air resounded with their battle cries. The forests burst into flame, and the rivers boiled, and at last the Titans were thrown into a lake of fire. With that the Olympic gods divided the world among themselves.

It was in the time of Zeus that mortal men began to test their powers.

TANTALUS, King of Argos, was a mortal who boasted that he was the son of Zeus. He was, indeed, the intimate of the gods, and if ever they showed honor to a human, it was to him. It was his custom, often, to ascend Olympus where the gods dwelt beyond the clouds; he went up alone and would come down his face transfixed with ecstasy and pride.

"I have dined on the mountain with my kin, the gods. I have eaten of ambrosia and drunk of the celestial nectar."

It began to be whispered throughout all of Hellas that Tantalus considered this honor to be his by right; that he grew more and more to consider himself the equal of the immortals.

"What proof is there?" his enemies—and in time even his friends, angered by his pride—demanded.

Then Tantalus spread a mighty banquet for his friends and served forth food so exquisite and strange that they were all amazed. "It is the food of the gods," Tantalus proclaimed. "I myself carried it from Mount Olympus when the deities were wine-entranced and could not see."

This news made brave men tremble. The food of the gods, as all men knew, conferred immortality on those who ate it and was therefore forbidden to the lips of humans. Moreover, to betray the trust of the host-guest relationship, as Tantalus had done by thievery, was a deed most heinous.

Tantalus added further to his sacrilege. He had in his possession a golden dog, entrusted to him by his friend Pandareus. "Keep this for me, and ask not how it came into my hands. It is the Guardian, wrought by Hephaestus god of the forge, that protected the infant Zeus."

When Pandareus came later to reclaim his prize, Tantalus, with bland face, swore a mighty oath.

"By Zeus himself, I have not what you ask. I know nothing whatever of the matter!"

Even more terrible was the deed men whispered of in secret in the dead of night. Tantalus was the father of three children, Pelops, Broteas and Niobe. It was observed that the youth Pelops had disappeared. He was most fair, a golden youth, given to sporting in the waves by his seaside home. Some said the god Poseidon fell in love with him and carried him away. But others murmured of a darker fate.

Tantalus, it was said, so honored by the gods, was privileged even more. The gods deigned to gather at his table, and to eat with him a mortal meal. It was a meal such as neither men nor gods had ever known!

What his motives were, were never known. It might have been a compulsion to offer to the gods the dearest thing he owned. Or—as men suspected—a desire to test the gods' omniscience and give means to gloat over them in private. Be that as it may, the tale held that Tantalus took his own son, Pelops, and he slew him, and as the water bubbled over the fire he sliced the youth's body into it, limb by limb. And during the second course of that god-honored meal, the slaves portioned out the cannibal meat for them to eat.

As the scent of the steaming bowl reached the gods' nostrils, they were aware that something was hideously wrong. They refused to eat, all except Demeter who was preoccupied with grief over her own lost daughter. Distractedly she took a bite from the loathsome dish. As soon as the youth's flesh touched her lips, she knew, and her face turned pale with horror.

Tantalus toppled from his throne, brought down by all his sins. In death he suffered the torments of the damned, standing forever in water that, should he thirst, instantly receded upon his stooping to it. Around him, trees bent with the weight of luscious fruit, but when hunger drove him to reach out, the branches rose beyond his reach. And always a huge stone balanced precariously above his head, ever on the verge of falling on him. Thus he was forever tantalized.

From Tantalus sprang the passion and pride that were to be the curse of all his seed.

II · THE GENERATION
OF PELOPS

PELOPS was the first to feel the curse, though he felt it less than others. After the terrible feast from which Demeter had shrunk back, retching, the gods assembled the pieces of Pelops' body. All were there, save his left shoulder, which had been consumed. The gods made for him a shoulder of pure ivory, and Rhea breathed into him again the breath of life. When he was once more seen on earth, he was of such beauty that all knew he had been given the blessings of the gods.

When Pelops came into manhood, and down covered his darkening chin, he bethought himself of a bridal. It was for Hippodamia, the far-famed daughter of Oenomaus, King of Pisa, that he longed. Lovely she was beyond compare, so lovely that her father could not bear the thought of losing her to another man. He feared, too, with the Cronos-fear that haunts all men: the knowledge that as they have replaced their fathers, so will they in turn be supplanted by their children's children. So Oenomaus, dreading both the loss of a too-loved child and the thought of being outshone by her issue, decreed that Hippodamia should wed only that man who could overcome him in a chariot race.

8

Oenomaus gave each suitor a head start, while he himself offered sacrifice to Zeus. Should Oenomaus be outraced, he would die, and throne and daughter pass to the winner. But Oenomaus' horses were so swift that none were their equal; they were reputed to be the gift of the God of War. So always, Oenomaus overtook the challenger and flung his spear into the hapless suitor's back. And Hippodamia the fair remained un-wed.

This was the maiden on which Pelops, son of Tantalus, set his heart. He went alone to the grey sea in the darkness, and he cried out to Poseidon, whom he knew loved him.

"If that dear love you bear to me can bring me good, hold back, I beseech you, Oenomaus' brazen spear. Let the swiftest of chariots bear me on the course. The danger is great and calls not to a coward. But each of us one day must die, and why should I wait for old age, unhonored, giving up my yearning for all lovely things? For me the ordeal calls, and I beseech you, give me godly aid and the issue I desire."

Thirteen heads had Oenomaus already nailed to his palace door. Hippodamia pined for the experience of love, but dared not give way to it, lest the object of her affections die. But when rumors of the approach of a young stranger reached her, she looked out from the roof of her father's palace and suc-cumbed.

"Truly," she thought, "this Pelops is the fairest among men, the beloved of the gods! His chariot of gold could skim the waves; his horses themselves have wings!" They must be the gift of Poseidon, her heart told her, pounding. Surely that meant the Olympians themselves had blessed his suit! But to make sure, she went to Myrtilus, her father's charioteer, and offered him a reward if he would betray her father.

Pelops also did not trust to the beneficence of the gods alone. He, too, bribed Myrtilus, asking him to remove a pin from the axle of the royal chariot. Half of Oenomaus' kingdom, which would be his through Hippodamia, was the price he offered. And Myrtilus, dazzled, replaced the pin in the wheel with one of wax.

All those of Oenomaus' city came out to watch the race, and it was not Hippodamia alone who longed for the youth to win or pitied the death he would die if he did not. As was the custom, Pelops started first, and his horses were fleeter than any of his predecessors'. For once Oenomaus was alarmed; he laid his whip again and again on his horses' backs, and narrower and narrower grew the gap between the chariots. They were almost even; they were abreast, and Oenomaus' arm was raised to fling the death-dealing spear.

Then it happened. The wheel flew off. Oenomaus was flung from his chariot and, tangled in the reins, dragged to his death. Before oblivion came he flung out a curse upon his servant Myrtilus who had betrayed him.

So Pelops brought down the strength of Oenomaus, gained his throne, and took Hippodamia to the bridal bed. He ruled all the kingdom in Oenomaus' stead, and in him grew both passion and pride.

In time, Myrtilus came to him in private to claim his reward, the half the kingdom promised. But Pelops laughed. "What need had I of you, when Poseidon dotes on me, when I could rely on my own skill and on my youth?"

So that the bribe would never become known, he hurled Myrtilus into Poseidon's sea. In that drowning moment, Myrtilus knew that the curse Oenomaus had put upon him had been fulfilled. And from the waves he flung his own curse back on Pelops.

UPON PELOPS' BROTHER and sister greater darkness fell. First Broteas insulted Artemis. He refused to perform the rites all men celebrated in honor of the goddess, boasting that he had no need to fear her power, that nothing could harm him, not even the sacred fire. As he grew in arrogance, he grew in madness, and in time, believing himself a god and thus immortal, he threw himself into the fire and was consumed.

Niobe, sister to Pelops and Broteas, seemed at first to be spared the family burden. She was wed to Amphion, the incomparable Musician-King of Thebes, and their marriage was greatly blessed by love. It was blessed, too, with children. Seven sons had been born to her, brave and beautiful, and seven daughters, the fairest of the fair. They grew up around her, filling her with pride till she lost that awe which wiser mortals feel toward the divine.

It was the custom in Thebes for all the women to make offerings to Leto, who had borne the twins Apollo and Artemis to Zeus. They poured oblations to her and wove garlands and sang their hymns.

"Greatest art thou among women,
deserving of honor,
because thy children excel all other children. . . ."

In the heart of Niobe, envy burned. One day, overcome, she flung down the garlands that she carried.

"From this day on, let the women of Thebes leave off devotion to Leto and worship me! She was mortal as I am mortal, but a homeless wanderer, disgraced by her conception until tiny Delos consented to take her in. I am queen of a great and fruitful kingdom. She was cursed by Hera, by whom I have been blessed. I am descendant of Olympian gods and of the Titans. I blaze in beauty like the sun. I am loved by a king who is great in wealth and power, who unlike Leto's lover Zeus is faithful. *I* have seven sons and seven daughters, she had one and one. Make your sacrifices to me, not Leto, for it is my power that shields the women of Thebes from harm!"

Her words, in their terrible arrogance, rang through the

heavens. Terrible was the answer they provoked. How did it happen? None of the dumbstruck watchers knew for sure, but afterwards they were to say the sun blazed with a blue-white fire, and the moon appeared until the sky became too bright to gaze upon. From within that blaze in the sky came arrows by which the children of Niobe were struck down. Seven youths and seven maids one moment stirred with young, warm life, the next were dead.

Niobe herself sank down motionless beside them, frozen in stony grief, dumb as stone and her heart like stone within her. Only her tears flowed in an endless fountain.

III · THE GENERATION OF ATREUS

THREE SONS had Pelops by Hippodamis—Atreus, Thyestes and Pittheus. The first two were the first of the seed of Tantalus to come to Mycenae of the Lion Gate. Perseus built it, so the legends say. His grandfather was Acrisius, King of Argos. When an oracle told him that his daughter would bear a son who would kill him, he locked up his daughter, Danae, so she could know no man and bear no child. But nonetheless she did bear a son—conceived, she said, by Zeus, who came to her in a shower of golden light. That son Perseus did kill his grandfather, all unaware, with a discus throw.

Eventually, Perseus became ruler of Tiryns of the yellow gold. While on his way to Tiryns, he was overcome by thirst. He stooped and plucked a mushroom and drank water from its heart. He was so pleased at this nectar that he raised up a city to mark the spot: Mycenae, named for the mushroom, *mykos*. Its rose-red towers floated like an illusion against the blue-bright sky, and the Cyclopes themselves built the city walls.

High upon its mountain top Mycenae dreamed, and crossing the spiral entry ramp a great gate rose, holding apart the walls of monolithic stone. The Lion Gate, for in its keystone triangle two lions raised proud heads on either side of an altar upon which their front paws rested. Mycenae—city of the lion's progeny, the lion's pride.

To Mycenae, Atreus and Thyestes came when, years later, they fled their father Pelops. Sthenelus, son of Perseus, who was now king, received them, and Eurystheus, Sthenelus's heir, befriended them, and when Eurystheus died Atreus and Thyestes were his heirs.

Atreus possessed a golden lamb, which he claimed authorized whoever owned it to be king. But Atreus was under oath, taken when he beseeched Artemis to help him gain the throne, to sacrifice the finest of his flock to her. He did slaughter the lamb, but had it stuffed and mounted, so that it continued to be for him the bestower of the royal power.

Thyestes, his brother, coveted the power, and thus the golden fleece. He coveted, too, Aerope, his brother's wife. Aerope lay with him and conspired to deliver into Thyestes' hands the lamb of power, and Thyestes was acknowledged by the people of Mycenae to be their king.

Atreus, when he discovered all that had happened, swore Thyestes should pay as no man had ever paid. He recalled his ancestor Tantalus' ghastly banquet and fell prey to visions. When, through a struggle that marked forever Mycenae's walls with fire, he gained back the throne, he feigned a desire for reconciliation with his brother. He invited Thyestes to a banquet, and Thyestes came.

In the dromos, or great hall, a splendid feast was spread. There, where the walls were painted with bright pictures of the family's valor, where fire leaped up from the central hearth that served as family altar, couches rimmed the room. For each guest, a table of his own was set. Slaves brought forth bowls and platters, gold-adorned, and the scent of the grape mingled with the savory fragrance of the roasted meats.

Before Thyestes, to show him honor, a special dish was

placed, meat and herbs together, chopped small. Thyestes ate. At the bottom of the dish he found small feet and fingers.

His cry of nausea and dismay rang out, and it was then that Atreus, eyes glittering, signalled a platter to be carried in.

He had seized Thyestes' sons and butchered them like lambs. It was their own flesh, limb and rib and heart, their father had eaten. He beheld, now, the remnants of the bodies, and their poor young faces. This was the host's-gift, which, at his own hearth, Atreus gave to his guest, his brother.

Vomiting murdered flesh, Thyestes fell from his couch with one deep groan. His foot sent the table crashing wide.

"So crash to ruin all the house of Tantalus!"

That was how came upon the house the final curse.

ATREUS WAS KING, and Thyestes had no power. Aerope for whom Thyestes had so disastrously lusted was now dead, drowned by her husband's hand. Nothing mattered to Thyestes then but revenge.

He sought an oracle, and the oracle foretold that he would be avenged by a son begat on his own daughter. This was to the Greeks a fearsome horror, but not to Thyestes in his frenzy. Nor did he care that she was virgin, scarce out of childhood, and dedicated to be a priestess in Athene's temple.

He went in secret to the land of Sicyon, where she dwelt, and lay in wait. When the girl, Pelopia, in dark of night went to make offerings to Athene, Thyestes seized and raped her. In the blackness, in her own blind terror, she did not even recognize her father's face. But as the brutal body crashed down upon her she managed to grab hold of her assailant's sword.

When she regained consciousness, the sword was still beside her, the design of its hilt imprinted in her hand. Thyestes, in his haste to escape undetected, had run off without being aware that it was gone.

Pelopia, sobbing in pain and shame, hid the sword near the

goddess's altar and invoked her aid. But soon her body began to swell with the child of that unholy union.

Shortly thereafter, Atreus himself came to Sicyon seeking for his brother, for an oracle had commanded that he restore Thyestes to Mycenae to avoid a famine in the land. Atreus saw Pelopia and loved her, and she was given to him by the King of Sicyon in marriage. When her son was born, Atreus joyfully assumed it was his own.

He named the boy Aegisthus. As the boy grew, belying the prophecies, Mycenae flourished. But its very stones bore witness to the ruling family's bloody acts. In the night, the superstitious said, one could hear murdered children weeping. And then after eight years the famine the oracle had predicted fell upon the land of Argos.

Atreus was torn between his public and his private duty—to bring Thyestes home was to court his own doom; not to bring him was to watch his people die.

His sons by Aerope, Agamemnon and Menelaus, were now in the full flower of their youth. He sent them on a quest to find Thyestes and to bring him home in chains, and so they did. Atreus wished his brother dead; he also wished that no more family blood should fall upon his hands.

In the night when the chained Thyestes for the first time slept again within Mycenae's walls, Atreus woke his youngest child, the lad Aegisthus.

"You are of the seed of the Lion Gate and must have a lion heart. If you can plunge this sword into our prisoner's heart, you shall be a man indeed."

It was the sword dedicated to Athene, which Pelopia had brought to Argos in her dowry.

Aegisthus was but seven years of age. In pride and fear, he crept through the painted corridors of the palace. By flaring lamplight, he found the prisoner sleeping. He must be brave. He lifted the sword in both of his small arms and held it high.

Was it some sound he made, or some nightmare vision? Thyestes cried and stirred and opened burning eyes to look up into a child's frenzied face and an upraised sword.

His sword. The sword lost eight years before, in dark of night, in committing a deed that dared not speak its name.

It all poured out then, from the terrified child—how he had been charged by Atreus with this mission. How the sword was dedicated to Athene and to his mother's honor. Thyestes knew then that this was the promised son who would avenge him. He sent Aegisthus for his mother. And Pelopia, hurrying through night-silent corridors, learned for the first time who it was who had destroyed her innocence and honor.

She plunged the sword into her own breast in her horror.

Thyestes, telling Aegisthus only that he was his true father, sent the boy to Atreus with the bloody sword, as proof that he, Thyestes, himself was dead.

When dawn came, Atreus with joy and thanks offered sacrifices by the sea. While he was at his prayers, Aegisthus and Thyestes fell on him and killed him.

Thyestes became king. In time Thyestes died. Aegisthus, now a young man, sought the throne. But Agamemnon sought the aid of Tyndareus, King of Sparta, and with his help became the ruler of the city of the Lion Gate.

Aegisthus fled.

AGAMEMNON

II

IV · AGAMEMNON

TYNDAREUS of Sparta had four children, so he thought. He did not know that after the first son and daughter had been born, his queen Leda had one night been visited in vision by a gigantic swan. The swan song that rang in her ears that night was a voice divine, and in her heart ever after she cherished a conviction that the twin boy and girl born to her from it were from the seed of Zeus.

Clytemnestra, the elder of Leda's daughters, was all dark fire. Her eyes blazed; she held herself tall and proud. Agamemnon on first sight of her desired her, recognizing instantly a pride and passion equal to his own. He asked Tyndareus to give her to him in marriage as a treaty-gift.

While Agamemnon, in this Spartan visit, was obsessed by this dark beauty, his brother Menelaus' eyes were all for the younger girl. Scarce out of childhood, yet voluptuous, she was like her twin brother—as fair as gold, already marked with a power infernal or divine. Menelaus wooed and won her and became Tyndareus' heir. And in time he reigned as King of Sparta.

In Mycenae, Agamemnon stood on his mountaintop with his

arm about his queen, and the high air that filled his lungs was intoxicating.

"Truly, we of the House of Atreus are little lower than the gods!"

Clytemnestra, standing tall beside him, felt her breasts swell with pride. They were exposed by her tight basque, in the Minoan-born Mycenean custom, and their rise and fall stirred necklaces of gold. Gold hung upon her ears, her hands, and gold was the embroidery she had exquisitely wrought upon her husband's cloak. Surely, not even the gods had skills or wealth surpassing this! Surely no god could surpass in virility or power her royal husband! Here in Mycenae, no longer a dark shadow at her sister's side, she knew her beauty took men's breaths away.

In the Spartan sun, Menelaus gazed fatuously on his wife and went from youth to middle age, as she grew bored. He did not know, as Clytemnestra did, the title that had been given to the younger woman when her fatal beauty first unfolded: *Helen the Despoiler*.

Agamemnon. Menelaus. Two men of the seed of Tantalus, of the House of Atreus of the Lion Gate. Bearing in blood and bone the family curse of pride and passion.

Clytemnestra. Helen. Sisters dark and fair, whose passions and pride were the equals of any men.

They were giants in the earth, and they cast long shadows.

V · APPLE OF DISCORD

OR A TIME, the curse slumbered. The breezes blew in peace across the mountaintop, and sunlight blazed in the intoxicating air. It was from the gods that the next troubles came.

As men later told it, the seeds of discord were sown at a wedding feast. Peleus, king of the Myrmidons in Thessaly, was being married to the beautiful sea-nymph, Thetis.

The wedding was taking place upon Mount Peleon, and the Olympian gods, seated upon their thrones, looked on and gave their blessings. It was a wedding looked on with favor by Hera, wife of Zeus. The muses sang and fifty nereids danced and splendid indeed were the gods' gifts to the bridal pair. For a time, as laughter rang and wine flowed, all was harmony—and with good reason. Hera, wishing to assure Thetis' joy, had caused Eris, goddess of discord, to be omitted from the list of guests.

The nuptials were at their height when Eris learned she had been omitted. Swift through the skies she sped and flung down at Peleus' side a missile deadly in its potential power.

It rolled to a stop among the celebrants—so small a thing, a golden apple, and tied to its stem a legend: *For the Fairest.*

The words were read, and a rippling murmur spread through

23

the throng. The prudent drew back quickly; women whose beauty was greater than their rank discreetly veiled their faces.

There were three women who by birth, station, beauty, each assumed the apple was for her: Athene, grey-eyed goddess of wisdom; Aphrodite, that alluring patroness of love; Hera herself. As one, they turned to Zeus, the arbiter supreme. In each exquisite face a glance flashed warningly, and for once Zeus, so often imprudent where women were concerned, was wise.

"I, who have known so much beauty, cannot choose which of three different types could be most fair. Go you to one yet innocent. There is on Mount Ida a young man reputed a great, impartial judge of women's beauty. You will find him a shepherd, watching o'er his flocks."

With one accord, the goddesses sped upon the wind to eastern Troy. There they found him—a shepherd, yes, but a king's son also; Paris, prince of Troy. He sat among his flocks in the drowsy heat of an Eastern afternoon, playing upon his pipes and dreaming dreams. Suddenly the air around him rang with music, the light changed shade and texture, and when his dazzled eyes again could see, he was surrounded by three exquisite beings from whose celestial garments perfumes drifted.

He, Paris, was to judge among the greatest of all women! Great was this honor, and great the lures which each of the lovely goddesses offered him.

"I shall give you power," Hera murmured. "You shall be lord of all Asia."

"You shall have great victory in war," the grey-eyed goddess said.

But Aphrodite whispered, "The most beautiful woman in all the world shall be your bride."

He was full of the arrogance of inexperience. He gave the golden apple, without a moment's thought, to Aphrodite. Thus he brought down upon himself and all the Trojans the implacable hatred of Hera and Athene; thus he set in motion a bloody contest that was to shake the world, not of the mortals only, but of the gods. This he did not know, nor would he have cared about it, on that dream-drugged afternoon.

THE FAIREST of mortal women was Leda's daughter Helen, she who was already wife to Menelaus.

Paris, dreaming of the exquisite prize that had been promised him, dreaming of Grecian women reputed to far surpass those of Troy, volunteered for a mission across the sea. Hesione, sister of King Priam, had some years before been carried off by Telamon, brother of that Peleus who had married Thetis. The Greeks had refused to return her to her homeland. He would go to negotiate, Paris offered. The Greeks had insulted Troy; honor must be restored; this was a mission suited for the testing of the manhood of a Trojan prince. In vain his prophetess sister Cassandra raised her warnings. In all eagerness, Paris sailed away.

In Sparta, Menelaus, the king, received the young man kindly. He gave ear to the justice of Paris' cause and entertained him royally for nine days. For nine days Helen, who had long since grown bored with Spartan starkness, offered the royal wine bowl to the dazzled youth. Her speech was decorous, but from her mouth came the honey breath of invitation. For nine nights Paris, in torment, lay upon his couch and could not sleep. Thinking of the dangers of dishonoring one's host. Thinking of the justice in kidnapping a Grecian queen in response for a Trojan princess earlier taken. Thinking of Aphrodite's promise, and the more potent promise in Helen's eyes.

On the tenth day, so confident in his own pride that he ignored what was obvious to all, Menelaus sailed to Crete to attend a kinsman's funeral, leaving kingdom and honored guest in Helen's charge.

That night, under cover of blackness, a royal ship raised furtive sails and set its course into the east. That night on deck, where soft breezes caressed bare skin, Paris did not sleep alone.

Great was the outcry when Menelaus returned to find his golden swan had flown her cage. Throughout all of Greece the war cry rang. Menelaus was making claim to an oath all Helen's suitors had sworn before Tindareus; that all who were rejected pledged themselves to uphold the sanctity of the marriage she had made. Through all of Hellas, men so sworn must rally now on Menelaus' aid.

Agamemnon sent embassies to Troy demanding Helen's safe return, but Troy refused. So great was her allure that all the Trojans, even old King Priam, had fallen beneath her spell. Besides, there was the matter of Hesione still unresolved. Abduction for abduction, and none but her uxorious husband believed Helen had been ravished against her will.

Soon, throughout east and west, preparations for war were underway. In both lands women, watching with resentful eyes, whispered that Helen and honor were excuses only. Peace had reigned long; young men dreamed of adventure, and those who felt youth slipping from their veins longed for one more chance for glory. In Troy, Cassandra, seeing her dark visions, warned of fire consuming topless towers. In Hellas, wise Odysseus, content with wife and newborn son, remonstrated that unfaithful Helen was not worth the price. All in vain. Everywhere, men's hearts became drunk with expectation, with desire for battlefield camaraderie and the clash of arms. And in the heavens, the gods and goddesses fanned their restlessness.

No band of men ever gathered would surpass the ranks of that royal army when the ships set sail; none was its equal save that noble troup who went with Jason to claim the Golden Fleece. Odysseus was there from Ithaca, and Idomeneus, King of Crete. The aged Nestor arrived from Pylus with his sons. Telemonian Ajax commanded a fleet from Salamis. Tlepolemus, son of Heracles, brought ships from Rhodes. Others there were too numerous to name, among them the great Achilles, offspring of Peleus and Thetis. And in Agamemnon, the pride and passion that was his family's strength, surged to a lusty life.

Clytemnestra, in the privacy of their nuptial couch, protested fervently his leaving Mycenae, throne, and children. Iphegenia, their first-born, exquisite and doe-eyed, was approaching marriageable age. Electra, the next child, barely knew her father. Orestes, the youngest, was still at the breast. She whispered at last what otherwise she would never say aloud: that her sister Helen had sensuality without sense, and as such was curse, not blessing, to any man who craved her. Helen the Despoiler, was not worth the havoc that followed in her wake.

Agamemnon laughed. "Childhood jealousy clouds your judgement. Do not fear; it is no woman's sweetness that draws me from your side. No, it is a sweetness more enduring. Who conquers Troy will be the greatest among men."

He did not say, *The equal to the gods.* She did not say, *Beware the family curse.* She did not say that her pride suffered when Helen's rescue beckoned so brightly to Agamemnon's eyes. That a woman's body could ache in the night when her man was gone. That all the passions of the House of Atreus burned within her, too.

So Agamemnon, in a splendor of bronze armor and purple plumes, marched with his army out through the Lion Gate. They left behind them women, children, slaves, the old men who were unfit to fight. They left behind a queen with a young child at her breast, her head high, her brain teeming with bitter thoughts toward her wayward sister.

On the ramparts of the palace walls, two figures watched. Iphegenia, closest to her parents' hearts, just entering into womanhood, gazed down at her father and dreamed of wedding such a man. And by her side Electra, small and dark, beheld her awesome father as a god.

VI · A WIND FOR TROY

T HE SCENE in the harbor of Aulis was worthy of the gods. Over a thousand ships, full-armed and manned, gathered there. And at their head, greatest among equals, was Agamemnon, son of Atreus. He strode along the rocky shore, watching as men polished armor and played war games and sang. And his pride blazed high.

The day came when all the preparations were complete, when ships and men chafed restlessly to be underway. Nothing remained but to seek the gods' blessing on the enterprise.

It fell to Agamemnon, as the acknowledged leader, to make the sacrifice. Afterwards, he never knew what precise thoughts ran through him as he stood poised on the sand beside the upheld sacrificial ram, his knife raised high. *Had* he blasphemed, thinking of other things? Or worse, thinking invocation of immortal aid unnecessary—or already guaranteed—since *he* was there? His arm swept down, and the hot blood gushed from the severed arteries onto the altar stones. And as it did, a serpent darted out from the nearby rocks. Its blue scales, all marked with crimson, dazzled in the sun as it coiled up the plane tree at the altar's side.

There was in the plane tree's branches a sparrow's nest. Agamemnon, transfixed against his will, watched as with one swift thrust of head the serpent devoured the eight nestlings and the mother. A murmur like a sigh ran through the assembled troops. A moment's silence, then from the illustrious ranks came a shocked exclamation.

"The gods have spoken. *Look*. The serpent turns to stone!"

To his own dismay Agamemnon felt the skin on his arms begin to prickle. He turned involuntarily toward Calchas the seer, and Calchas, meeting his eyes, spoke quietly.

"It is no good omen. Nine. The number nine. Nine years of deaths before, in the tenth year, Troy will fall."

Did Agamemnon in that split second murmur disbelief? That was another of the things he wondered later in the unblessed nights. The sacrificial ritual was completed, but already the mood among the troops had changed as had the wind. It now blew north and would not carry them to Troy. An undercurrent of uneasiness ran among them, disguised by jokes and bragging and bravado. A day passed, and another, and another, and they could not sail for Troy. The ships sped instead on shorter trips along the coasts, ravaging cities, being swept apart by violent storms. They returned to Aulis, and men took out their restlessness in increasingly violent and daring sport.

So many things occurred, the tales became tangled and exaggerated in retelling, as such stories do. A soldier killed one of Artemis's sacred stags, boasting the goddess herself could not have done it better. Agamemnon killed a hare, which unfortunately was about to bear her young. There were other episodes. Agamemnon, sitting in his tent after the nightly military conferences were done, knew one thing only: The winds were wrong. The ships could not sail. Until the winds changed, they could not sail for Troy.

That was the only thing that was clear and sure. But day by day, other rumors reached his ears. Men grown devout by deprivation were muttering half-remembered prayers. Were gazing uneasily at entrails of butchered animals and at flocks of birds.

Some god had been offended. The source of the offense must be sought out and reparations made. And the responsibility lay always with the leader, for he who was highest was held accountable by gods and men for all that happened under him.

He, Agamemnon, must discover the cause of the gods' displeasure and must appease it, or he would lose all his authority.

He commanded Calchas the seer to make all things ready. He himself, before all the troops, would offer sacrifice, and Calchas would read the signs.

They stood again upon the beach in the still hot afternoon. Around them, ring on ring, the men stood silent—princes, demigods, kings, the flower of all Hellas. Those highest in rank, among them Menelaus, lifted the sacrificial animal high. It stood dumb, in that curious prescient way such victims often have, as Agamemnon performed the dedication, the libation on its brow. Again the knife flashed, and blood spurted smoking, and in a pressing stillness the body was flayed, quartered, gutted.

The entrails were cast forth. Calchas stepped forward; gazed at them. His skin was pale, his eyes opaque, as though the Underworld he gazed on was within.

The dark eyes lifted, staring straight at Agamemnon. Then, quietly, Calchas spoke.

"Complete the ritual; burn the sacred parts and divide the meat. What has been revealed is mystery so sacred it must be made known only to the Atrean kings."

The gaze of the two brothers met and locked. Without a word they turned and strode toward Agamemnon's tent, and Calchas followed. Having entered, he dropped the tent flap shut behind him. It was dim here, after the brightness of the afternoon. Agamemnon swung round, his voice brusque with foreboding.

"What have you to say to us, Calchas the seer?"

There was a silence, and in it the younger man seemed to grow in stature. When he spoke, his voice was quiet. "Words I would give anything not to speak, son of Atreus."

The title hung in the air with the weight of the old curse.

"Come to the core of it," Menelaus said impatiently. "You saw something in the entrails. What?"

"That Artemis has been offended deeply, and the burden rests upon the Mycenean king. There will be no wind for Troy until his daughter Iphegenia is offered in sacrifice."

Outside the skin-walled tent, the sounds of the ritual went on in the blazing sun.

Agamemnon spoke hoarsely. "Tell Talthybius to let the trumpet blare. Disband the army. I will never bring myself to kill my daughter."

Menelaus' face darkened. "You swore an oath to uphold your brother's honor. You formed this army for that great cause. Will you now betray them, me, and your word?"

"I gave no word to kill my child—"

"You have other children," Menelaus said brutally. "You will no doubt have more. Our honor, and the honor of all Hellas, we have but once. Shall the barbarians of the East think Greece is theirs for pillaging without punishment. Shall men think they may rape other men's wives with impunity? *Look at me!*"

Calchas discreetly slipped away unnoticed.

Agamemnon's eyes blazed. "You expect me to show dread of you, I who am sprung from Atreus the undreading?"

"I expect you to be firm of mind! Have you forgotten with what strong ambition you yearned to be leader of leaders in this expedition? Oh, you feigned reluctance, but your heart was eager! How you touched every man's right hand; how the door of our father's palace was unbarred for any citizen who wished to enter! And here at Aulis, how you sought public favor! But since you gained generalship, that wind indeed has died. You are difficult of access, even to me. Lackeys preserve the privacy of your exalted rank! And when the army stirred uneasily, when they grew tired of waiting and would go home, what an unhappy face you showed! *Then* you sought me out. 'Brother, what shall I do? What way can I find? I will pay any price.' Not that your concern was for my wife, my honor. *No,* to keep you from being deprived of your command and your chance for glory! Now the price has been named, and you don't wish to pay it!"

With difficulty Agamemnon kept his voice within control. "Easy words for you to say. It is not *you* who has been asked to pay the price."

"No! It is *you!* Has it not even occurred to you, brother, to wonder why?"

The pictures sprang into Agamemnon's mind. Himself long ago in Sparta, in the rash exuberance of youth, promising to Artemis, if his suit for Clytemnestra succeeded, the fairest gift to come to him within the year. Himself, when the newborn daughter was placed in his arms for his acknowledgement, laughing denial of regret that she was not a boy. Proclaiming Iphegenia the fairest gift to have come his way. Not even thinking of the goddess or her aid. Feeling already that wife, child, throne were his by his own deserving. For was he not Agamemnon of the Lion Gate?

The pride of the House of Atreus, which thought itself the equal to the gods.

The tent rang with silence, and in that moment Menelaus knew that he had won.

VII · THE BEACH AT AULIS

W HEN THE LETTER reached Clytemnestra, her heart
blazed with pride.

Achilles, as you know, we sought as our companion in
this glorious venture because the oracles warned we should
have no success without him. He is heir to Peleus, warrior
without peer, the most golden of all the golden youth.
Many are the houses who have sought him for their daughters, but it is upon ours that his choice has fallen. He re-
fuses to sail with us to Troy unless a bride of our house
goes to Phthia. *I bid you then, send Iphegenia at once to
Aulis.*

Great was the rejoicing throughout all Mycenae. Lamps
burned into the night as slaves spun and wove and sewed, and
chests were packed. Clytemnestra, supervising the splendors of
the preparations, was impatient with time spent in nursing the
infant Orestes at her breast. If only she could have turned him
over to a slave, as other high-bred women did! But no, Agamemnon had decreed that only royal milk should feed his royal
heir. So she held him automatically, feeling the tug of his eager

mouth upon the nipple, remembering with what joy and pride she had suckled Iphegenia her first-born. That joy was shadowed now at the awareness of how soon she must let this most-loved child depart from her. But that was the way of things for women.

At intervals during the bustle, Clytemnestra watched her daughter anxiously. What was she thinking, this child-woman whose body had barely swelled from the straight lines of girlhood, who such short years ago had prattled so busily at Clytemnestra's knee? As womanhood and grace had grown within her, she had grown quiet. She idolized her father. More than she does me, Clytemnestra thought, and put the awareness from her hastily.

At the last moment, when the horses were straining at their reins, she decided to accompany the bridal party. There was fierce scurrying within the palace, cries and blows as slaves did not pack her coffers with sufficient speed. Mycenae was impregnable; the inhabitants from humblest to the greatest stood in awe not of Agamemnon only, but of her. Surely the city-kingdom would be safe for a time without its royal rulers! And so, radiant with jewels, as splendid as a goddess in her embroidered cloak, she stood beside this dearest of daughters as the chariots swept toward the sea. Orestes she was obliged to have travel with her, for he could not be that long separated from her breast. Of Electra, that thin, plain inconvenience for whom a nurse could care, she did not think at all.

From the port, the ship all decked with flags set out for Aulis. Clytemnestra stood in the prow with the wind upon her face, watching the clouds scudding through the skies before them and almost feeling as though she, too, were bound for Troy. Iphegenia sat, her slim arms clasped around her knees, and thought with eagerness and fear of the nuptials and the bridal-bed and destiny. Thought of what it would be like to be the wife of a man such as the father she adored.

In Aulis, Agamemnon wrote, rewrote and ultimately sealed a letter to his wife.

I send this word to supplement my former message to you, seed of Leda. Do not send our child to waveless Aulis. Our daughter's wedding celebrations are indefinitely postponed.

He gave the letter to an old trusted slave in the dark of night, when the dog star Sirius was high in the heavens. But Menelaus, pacing on the sands, saw what was taking place. He seized the letter, opened it and read it, and so the message granting her reprieve did not reach Iphegenia, who was all unaware.

When word of this circumvention reached Agamemnon, he was filled with rage, and the quarrel between the brothers blazed anew. But now a new goad arose to trouble his divided mind.

He could meet Iphegenia secretly and send her back. The waiting troops did not yet know Calchas' reading of the oracle. They need never know.

Ah, but could he trust that? The whole breed of prophets is rotten with ambition, Agamemnon thought bitterly. One day Calchas would speak out.

Not if he died first. That would be so easy.

But what of Menelaus, who was determined that they go to Troy?

What of Odysseus, so temperate and wise, equal to them in rank? Odysseus had been watching him with level eyes of late. Perhaps he already knew. Or would find out. Or guess. Agamemnon could see him, standing up in the midst of all the Argives, telling the whole truth about the oracles, telling how Agamemnon had promised this sacrifice to Artemis and had then played false.

No! He could not bear it. No daughter, however fair, was worth that dishonoring, that loss of place. Especially now, on the brink of this great expedition that could wipe out forever the dark stain upon the honor of the House of Atreus.

A running of feet. A messenger bursting in.

"King of all Hellenes, I bring you word that the daughter whom you call Iphegenia has arrived. And with her your heir, Orestes, and his mother, the noble daughter of Tyndareus."

Clytemnestra. Clytemnestra here. What could he say to her, with what face greet her? She has undone me, Agamemnon thought heavily. He had troubles enough already. But he ought to have known, oughtn't he, that she would come? It was a mother's right to deck the bride.

Suddenly the weight of the family curse was heavy on him.

THE LAST PART of the women's journey had been made by land, for in the harbor no wind stirred to carry vessels out or in. They had put to shore some distance off and sped in chariots across the sand. Everywhere the land was fair with springtime, and flowers blossomed among the sparkling rocks. The holy stillness of Artemis' sacred grove . . . the army's stronghold with the many-colored tents and crowd of horses. . . . Iphegenia was half in a trance, but Clytemnestra's eyes took all in eagerly. Truly, this was a host of men equal to the gods! Men polishing bronze armor, men sitting talking, men taking pleasure in complicated moves upon the draught board. Diomede delighting in the discus, and in the harbor a host of ships, the sight a pleasure honey-sweet.

On the shore a young man in full armor was racing with a four-horse chariot. The charioteer kept shouting, urging his gold-bridled horses with a goad. But the runner kept pace with them, lap for lap.

Clytemnestra laid a swift hand on Iphegenia's arm. "Daughter, look! That is he who will be your bridegroom, the great Achilles!"

She was untroubled by the bold stares that fell upon them, the murmurs of astonishment as they passed. For a high-born woman to dare the male world of an army camp was strange enough, but for her to bring a maiden so young and obviously untouched! Let them look, Clytemnestra thought recklessly. They will learn soon enough why we have come!

She spoke curtly to the charioteer. "Stop here, and send word to his majesty that we have arrived. We have had a long journey and will ease our feet in this fountain's gracious stream. The horses you may turn loose to browse on meadow grass."

Already a crowd was gathering. Clytemnestra accepted a proffered hand, stepped down delicately, and removed her sandals. She was pleasurably aware that while Iphegenia was the object of curious stares, it was upon she herself that eyes rested lustily.

She could hear the murmur spreading through the men. "Clytemnestra." "Agamemnon's queen, Tyndareus' daughter." And even more gratifying, "Helen's sister . . . if she too be this fair, no wonder Menelaus is stricken at his loss!"

Then, for these were men as fleet of intellect as of foot, "The daughter, too." "Did Agamemnon miss his daughter so much he had her fetched?" "Is there to be a wedding, and to whom?"

From the ring of watchers a voice spoke graciously. "Great is the blessedness of the great. Behold our leader's daughter, and Tyndareus's daughter Clytemnestra. Of what great houses are they sprung, and to what exalted fortune they have attained! So do the powerful and wealthy become as gods."

Clytemnestra turned toward the speaker with equal charm. "An omen of good do I count your greeting. My hope is that I come to be bride's matron for a happy marriage. From the carriages take the dower gifts I bring and carry them carefully to her father's tent. Iphegenia, stand here by your mother. Show to the world how happy is our house."

Iphegenia stirred as from a dream. The dark eyes gazed, bewildered. Then a soft sound escaped her, and like one of Artemis' own deer she was running fleet-footed towards the imposing figure that approached them.

Agamemnon. How swiftly she runs from me to him, Clytemnestra thought. But it's natural. She loves him most out of all the world. Well, may she one day run to her bridegroom with as much eagerness.

Iphegenia, clinging to her father's stalwart breast, had no thought now for any man but him. How long it seemed since she had seen him!

"I thank you, father, for bringing me to you," she murmured. The formal phrases did little to conceal the warmth that was in her heart.

"Perhaps your gratitude is right, perhaps not. I do not know."

The words were uneasy. Iphegenia searched his face. How strange he looked, as though some burden pressed on him. Of course; it was the war! She must remember that that must be his first preoccupation. Surely that was why his speech was so unlike himself, and in those clipped and cryptic sentences.

She made her eyes dance, in the way she knew from childhood beguiled him from his cares. "Away with your frown! Smooth your brow and make it friendly!"

"There! I am as happy as can be, you see?" Agamemnon made his face smile with effort, but it was no use. Iphegenia's hand came up, touching his cheek. The eyes in her young face were grave and questioning. "I grieve for the separation that must come between us," he said brusquely, and put her from him, turning to Clytemnestra. "Come into my tent. It will be cooler there, and you can rest."

It would be quiet there, and private, and he could think. Even Odysseus, even Menelaus would respect a man's reunion with his family. If only he could be sure that Calchas had not spoken.

He led the way to his flag-decked tent, his face a mask.

If he had thought his task would be easier there, he had been wrong. Iphegenia, sensing a sorrow she did not understand, sought to divert him with prattle of her wedding. And every word out of my mouth, Agamemnon thought bitterly, is fraught with double meaning that she does not know.

That she must know, soon. I shall be unable to put it off.

Menelaus, Calchas, Odysseus know too much for me to be able to postpone the sacrifice, prevent it. Not without the loss of everything I hold most dear.

A father ought to hold his daughter's life most dear.

Yet a king of kings ought to hold his country's honor and its welfare first.

A man. . . .

He became conscious of Clytemnestra watching him with burning eyes. She knows, he thought dully. Not what is wrong, but that something surely is. He met her gaze squarely, his head imperiously high, and her eyelids dropped. When she spoke, her voice was honey, asking of Achilles' lineage, of the nuptial plans.

It was her serpentine way of pursuing her will obliquely, which had always enchanted him. It terrified him now. Shorter and shorter grew his answers, until to his dismay he heard himself snapping, "You ought not to have come. I did not bid you come."

Her head jerked up. "It is my proper office to give my own child in marriage!"

"It is not proper for you to mingle with this mob of soldiery!"

" 'The flower of Hellas'? That is what their songs sing, do they not?" Clytemnestra's eyes flashed. "Do you not know by now I fear neither god nor man? I shall raise high the bridal torch—"

"I say you shall go home. You have responsibilities in Mycenae."

"No, by the Argive goddess! I have responsibility for my daughter and her wedding! You go and mind your war!"

It was no use. Nothing was any use. And so we learn, Agamemnon thought heavily, that we cannot avoid the family curse. Blood must pay for blood. He could do nothing but move straight ahead as the oracle had demanded, making himself deaf to all other voices.

He left the tent to seek out Calchas the oracle-priest, to tell him to proceed with the arrangements.

Clytemnestra stood looking after him, her brows contracted. After fifteen years' marriage, she could read him well, and his face had been the face of Tantalus.

Behind her Iphegenia, exhausted by their travels, had curled like a child on Agamemnon's couch and slept the sleep of innocence. But Clytemnestra could not rest, not until she had divined the cause of this uneasiness, which had been growing since first she set foot from the chariot. The men who had greeted her had been dumbstruck by her arrival. And their astonishment when she had spoken of the projected marriage. . . .

She drew back, for strange footsteps were approaching the tent at a brisk pace. The flap was thrust aside.

"Where is the general of the Achaeans?" The young man was not looking in her direction; he sensed her presence but was assuming her to be one of Agamemnon's minions, and he spoke curtly, obviously consumed with anger. "Here I am waiting weeks for a breath of wind and only with difficulty holding my troops in check. Does he not realize what a violent passion for this expedition has fallen upon all of these Hellenes? What am I to answer my men when they are constantly asking why we linger? Something must be done, or I must lead my army home and wait no more for the sons of Atreus."

It was Achilles. She knew him immediately, though he knew her not. She stepped forward, and Achilles turned with impulsive exclamation.

"By all modesty, what woman is this who possesses so ravishing a form?"

"I do not wonder you recognize me not. Hitherto we have been nothing to each other. I am Clytemnestra, Leda's daughter and Agamemnon's queen."

Achilles bowed hastily, coloring at the recollection of his familiar tone. "Lady, my respects. Forgive my intrusion. I shall withdraw, it being unsuitable for me to speak with you like this."

"Surely not, under the circumstances." Clytemnestra held her hand out, smiling. "Please do not leave. Join your right hand with mine as happy omen for your nuptials."

Achilles stared. "My nuptials? Is it some delusion that makes you speak so strangely?"

"It is natural, I suppose, for any man to be shy when he first meets his new kin before the wedding." Clytemnestra laughed graciously, as was suited a noble lady putting a young suitor at his ease. But the astonishment in his eyes communicated itself to her, and she faltered. Those eyes narrowed, and their sharp gaze swept the tent's interior, taking in the young girl asleep and vulnerable. When Achilles spoke again his voice was hard.

"I never sought your daughter in marriage, lady, and no talk of such has reached me from the sons of Atreus."

"*What?*" Had she been abused, Clytemnestra wondered; had she been dream-possessed? But no; the messenger who had brought Agamemnon's summons had been real. She said through stiff lips, "If I have been matchmaking where there is no match, I am mortified for myself and for my child."

"There is more to this than we yet know." Achilles bowed. "Farewell, lady, I shall seek out your husband and try to find the truth."

He strode toward the doorway, but before he could leave the flap was pushed open and an old man entered. A slave, by his garb and his demeanor, and it was no part of a slave's right to enter Agamemnon's chamber thus uninvited. But there was a desperate look upon his face, and a flicker of recognition stirred in Clytemnestra.

"You are of Tyndareus' household, are you not? You came to Mycenae as part of my dower gifts."

"Aye, lady, and have sought to serve you well. It is with you my loyalty lies, not with the king." The man fell down on his knees before her. One hand crept out as though to pluck her garments; drew back hastily. Clytemnestra bent to him.

"Do not be afraid to touch me if you wish something of me."

"I wish to do service for you, before too late. I must speak with you in private." Achilles moved to leave, and the slave cried shrilly, "Son of Thetis, stay! It is with you too that my mission lies. Oh, my lady, my queen, you must believe me, you know how I've served you, how I seek your interests."

It was Clytemnestra, now, who touched him, speaking gently to calm his evident terror. "Disclose whatever secret you have for me."

Stillness. A shudder. Then bare words blurted out. "The father that begot your child is going to kill that daughter with his own hand."

The stillness rang as though all of the stars had clashed together. Clytemnestra's hand caught the man's wrist in a grip of iron. "You are not sane!"

"It is your husband who has gone mad, toward you and your child. In all else but that he is quite sane. And it is in the name of reason that he will have her white throat slashed."

"*For what reason? What demon drives him to this?*" Already, a corner of Clytemnestra's brain observed, she was accepting the old man's words as truth. His terror spent now, he looked at her fearlessly.

"Because of the oracle. All the camp knows it, though the sons of Atreus only fear we do. Artemis has been offended, and the oracle says the virgin must be sacrificed or there will be no wind for Troy."

That was why he had sent for Iphegenia. That was why he did not want her, Clytemnestra, here. That was why Achilles had known nothing; he had been just a pawn. She saw his face color as the import of this insult struck him, but she could spare no thought for his feelings now. *Ah, my child, I have brought you here to your destruction. Yours, and mine.*

Clytemnestra, shaking, spun round to Achilles, dropping to her knees. "I feel no shame to kneel before you, for I am mortal and you born of a goddess. Child of Thetis, champion my distress and hers that was called your wife. For you I garlanded her and brought her here, to find Artemis' altar would be her bridal-bed. By your manhood, by your right hand, by your immortal mother, I beg you to protect us. It was your prestige that drew me here; your prestige can save us. I have no other place to turn for refuge."

Achilles spoke slowly, as though in thought. "My pride, like that of your house, runs high. I have learned with difficulty to temper both grief and joy. And I have sworn allegiance in this war to the leadership of the son of Atreus. But when that leadership is not good, I shall not obey. You have been treated wretchedly by him closest to you. And my name, being invoked in the matter, has been insulted. I swear that never shall your daughter, spoken of as mine, be slaughtered by her father. If I allowed it, I should be in part the cause." He put out his hands and drew her to her feet. "Lady, have courage. You see in me a god powerful to save you. If I am not one, then I shall become one. As I live, I shall save the girl."

The words came automatically to lips that still were numb. "May the gods bless you for helping us in our distress."

"Hear me now. You must try to persuade your husband to come to a better mind."

"Persuade!" Reason was returning to Clytemnestra's brain,

and her voice rang with contempt. "He is too proud to listen, and too much a coward to face the army if they know the truth."

"Some arguments carry more weight than others. Beseech him, by all that is holy to him, not to kill the child. If you persuade him, there will be no need for me to intercede. But if you succeed not, come to me. I shall keep watch, so you shall not be put to an unseemly search."

"So be it, then." Though he was young, his words were wise. And if there are gods, Clytemnestra thought, he being a righteous man will obtain their blessing. If there were none, it would be of no use for her to pray.

She bowed silently, acknowledging his leaving. Then she turned and saw through brimming tears a slight figure sitting upright, rigid, with all the terrors of Hades in her eyes.

Iphegenia had awakened and had heard it all.

VIII · IPHEGENIA

W HEN AGAMEMNON, armored against all private
doubt, left the grove of Artemis and returned to his
encampment, he found Clytemnestra standing before
the tent. So be it; the gods must have ordained as part of his
torment that he should prepare her. He cleared his throat.

"Child of Leda, I must speak with you apart from our daughter, of things that it is improper for brides to hear."

"What is the message for which you find this meeting so well
suited?"

Clytemnestra's words were temperate, but a fire burned behind them, and quite suddenly he knew he could not tell her.
He said abruptly, "Fetch the child to me. The lustral waters are
prepared, and the meal-cakes wait to be thrown in the cleansing
fire."

"And the victims whose dark blood must gush?" Clytemnestra stopped; turned toward the tent. She held the flap back
silently, and Iphegenia was there like a mute statue. So small
she looked, in the fine-spun dress woven for her bridal, and her
face as white as Artemis' own moon. Her eyes, intent on Agamemnon and unfaltering, were very dark.

45

Agamemnon went toward her, forcing down the thickness in his throat. "Child, where have all your smiles gone?"

Her eyelids dropped; a tremor ran through her, and she drew her mantle before her face. He made himself go on. "How now? You both conspire to show me faces of consternation?"

There was the barest perceptible movement, like a faint wind shifting, yet now Clytemnestra stood tall beside the trembling girl.

"Answer what I ask you like a man, husband. This child, yours and mine—are you going to kill her?"

The direct challenge, and the knowledge behind it, made him reel. He could only mutter, "What cruel words."

"Answer my question."

"Ask reasonable questions and you shall have reasonable answers." That was the way; cleave to the rational and stray not into the dangerous pits of human feelings. Sacrifice for the sake of the army was a rational demand.

"I ask one question only. Do you mean to kill her?"

By all the holy heavens, what wretched fate was his! Agamemnon did not know he spoke aloud, but Clytemnestra caught the words up quickly. "*And* mine, and *hers*. Agamemnon, I *know*."

The very trees of the hillsides waited for his answer, and his silence was itself confession.

Clytemnestra's hand dropped. "Hear me now, and let us have done at last with twists and riddles. You married me against my will. My father Tyndareus wanted your alliance, so you got me. And I became reconciled to you and was a blameless wife. I was temperate in my demands upon you in the marriage-bed, and I increased your house so that your comings in and goings out were filled with joy."

Inside the tent Orestes, forgotten, whimpered in his slumbers, and she jerked her head toward the sound. "I bore a son to you, after two earlier daughters. Of one of them now, you cruelly would bereave me. If someone asks you why you kill her, what will you say? Or must I say it for you? So that Menelaus may have Helen! You kill your own child to get back your brother's whore!"

"She is your sister," the ghost of Agamemnon's voice said through stiff lips.

"No less a harlot! And it may be I learn by her example! If you go off to Troy and leave me with no husband, how do you think my heart will feel? *And with no more daughter!*" The tears were streaming down her cheeks, but she paid no heed. "As I go through the echoing rooms and see the chairs all empty of her presence, I shall have nothing to occupy my mind but thoughts of this: He destroyed my child, the father that begot her. He heeded not her prayers, nor the importunings of his own wife, but laid her down for his own pride and honor, and to bring a harlot home from Troy! Tell me, husband, what sort of homecoming do you think this prepares for you?"

All at once something snapped within her, and she heard herself shouting out words that were not wise. "When you sacrifice that child, what prayers will you utter? What blessings ask for yourself against the dark ahead? Did you consider this, or is your only thought to parade your scepter and play the general?"

She saw Agamemnon's face darken, and she could say no more. She turned away blindly. "Iphegenia, speak."

Iphegenia closed her eyes and flung a frantic prayer to all the gods, but no guidance came. She wet her lips, and the voice that came through them was but thin whisper. "If I had all Orpheus' eloquence I could bewitch by words, but I have no art." She shuddered, the trembling that had been like faint tremors within her growing and growing until it engulfed her in an earthquake wave. Scarcely conscious of what she was doing, she fell forward into a heap at her father's knees.

The gods were merciful; that inner pain was swelling so that it blotted out all thought, even the terrible pictures that had been haunting her since the moment she had heard the old slave's words. She was aware of nothing but the wave of pain until she felt a faint touch like a breeze upon her tangled hair. Her father's hand, caressing her.

"I do love my children," Agamemnon said with difficulty. "Otherwise I should be mad. Horror there is for me if I do this thing; equal horror there is if I do not. There can be no voyage against Troy without this sacrifice. The prophet says so. I am greatest of all kings here in Aulis, and there rages a passion among our countrymen to sail with all speed for the barbarian land. If we do not, if the rape of Helen is not avenged, no woman will be safe in all of Hellas. They will be raped or killed by their own hearths; and I will be killed, if I heed not the oracle. It is Hellas for whom I must, whether I would or not, offer this sacrifice. The claim of country and its laws is the highest claim. We are Hellenes, and Hellas must be free and proud, as far as it lies with you or me to make her so."

He could say no more. He must gird himself to put on the harness of necessity. Agamemnon drew his hand back as though it had touched fire, and with a face like Ares himself he strode away.

They were left together, the two women, to face that which could not be spoken. Clytemnestra, feeling for the first time in life utterly forsaken, could do nothing but drop down herself, covering and warming Iphegenia with her own body.

This, was nightmare from which there was no waking. *Except for Achilles. He is our last best hope.*

Could even he stand against Agamemnon and the whole army?

A shadow fell across her, and she raised her head to see Achilles standing above them, sword in hand.

"Ah, daughter of Leda, most unhappy lady." He knew, already. And there *was* no hope. *Child, child, it is the end for us.*

Clytemnestra's arms tightened around her frail burden, but her voice was quiet.

"What is that clamor from the Argive hosts?"

"The demand for sacrifice. The whole camp is possessed by a frenzy. Naught is real, naught matters but a wind for Troy."

"And what did you say?"

"That they should not kill the bride that was meant for me."

What was their answer, Clytemnestra's eyes asked. In reply, Achilles held out an arm bloodied by pelting stones. *Even he. Even such as he cannot avert their lust for blood and war, or alter Fate's inexorable demands. This proud army is turned into a rabble that has become the curse upon our house.*

"I and my armor-bearers," Achilles said, "stand to prove this child will not be slaughtered with my consent."

There were so few, against so many. "What must I do?"

"Cling to your daughter, lady." He need not tell her that. Her arms tightened fiercely as though the slight figure were already being pulled away by the current of the Styx.

Feeling that pressure, Iphegenia stirred. The merciful mists of sense-dulling pain were now receding. Vaguely, like visions seen through altar smoke, pictures swam into focus in her mind's eye. The look on the old slave's face as he had blurted out the words. Her mother's figure growing suddenly so still. Like a statue; like a monument to grief. The expression of torment in her father's eyes. She had never seen him look like that before. He had never been torn like this before.

As from a great distance, she heard the beloved voice. *We are Hellenes.* That was both their sacred privilege and their sacred duty. And they were more. They were both, father and daughter, the offspring of Mycenae, the lion's pride.

What was the privilege and the duty of the lions' progeny at a time like this?

I must be in a trance, Iphegenia thought dizzily, for already to my nostrils comes the scent of incense and smoke of sacrifice.

Perhaps this is all dream from which I will soon awaken. Perhaps I have already died, and this is memory, memory, for I have not yet drunk merciful oblivion from the River Lethe.

I don't want to die. It is so sweet to look upon the light and the bright waters and meadows blooming with hyacinths and roses. But soon no longer will the light be mine. I am afraid to go alone into the unknown dark.

Though it was day, the dark was already pressing round her. She could feel the chill of death within her bones. But with it, in concurrent coursing, was warmth, and a silver glow like the moon made luminous the darkness.

The moon, Artemis' own blessing.

When she was small, she had thought that were she not a princess she would want to be a priestess of Artemis.

All at once, though she could feel Clytemnestra's body pressed to hers, hear Achilles' voice, she was in a clearing in a sacred grove. It was night, yet the silver light was bright as day. And the night rang with music. She was alone, yet not alone; she was enfolded in a divine presence more warm, more loving than anything she had ever known.

The goddess had come for her. And she knew, then, what must be.

Iphegenia drew a deep, shaking breath. The visions in her inner eye dissolved, and she was on her knees, looking up into the faces of her mother and Achilles.

"Mother, hear me." Her voice was quiet, but even to her own ears different. A new authority enveloped her like a sacred mantle. "I am resolved to die."

She had not known this in words until she heard them come from her own lips, yet it was true. She bowed her head, assenting.

A deep cry came from Clytemnestra's throat, and the maternal arms tightened like a band of iron. Iphegenia turned, smiling gently.

"Mother, don't you see? When the odds are impossible, resistance is folly. It has provoked your wrath against my father. It has brought suffering on our behalf to Achilles. The gods have spoken, and to accept the will of the gods with grace is always best."

She put a hand up to brush the dark hair back from Clytemnestra's face, and for the moment roles were reversed; she was the mother. "I am a princess. You bore me for the common good of Hellas, not for yourself alone. Nor is my life mine only. Ten thousand men have shields and oars in hands. Our country has been wronged. *They* have the courage to do brave deeds against the foe and to die for Hellas if that must be. Can I do less? I am of the pride of lions, and a Tyndarid woman. Another Tyndarid woman has by her beauty caused this trouble. Let me lay mine down to save Hellas, if I may."

Clytemnestra could not speak. It was Achilles who answered, deeply moved. "Child of Agamemnon, one of the gods meant to make me happy if I won you as my wife. Hellas is blessed in you, indeed."

He would not kill to save her. That pledge she had asked of him, and he had honored it, without need of words. She turned to Clytemnestra, her voice breaking. "Mother, do not weep. Do not make me a coward. Help me, *please.*"

Clytemnestra swallowed, and her back grew as firm as the pillars of stone that held Mycenae's gate. When she spoke, her voice was rigidly controlled.

"Speak, child. You will get justice from me."

"Promise me . . . afterwards . . . not to cut off your hair or wear black robes."

The eyes blazed. "You expect me not to mourn for you all my life?"

"The altar of Artemis will be my memorial. I have been blessed, Mother. I have been chosen to be benefactress of all Hellas."

Because your father is a coward, Clytemnestra thought viciously. She choked back the words. "Is there anything I can do for you?"

The words of the whisper stabbed her. "Do not hate my father."

"*By all the gods—*" She stopped again. "He shall have to run a fearful race because of you."

"He does not wish this," Iphegenia said gently. "It is for Hellas that he makes the sacrifice."

Yes, by treachery and cowardice.

There was a silence. Achilles had withdrawn, and they were alone. When Iphegenia spoke again, her voice was quite natural. "Someone must lead me to the sacred grove before men come to drag me."

"I will go with you."

"No. Not you!" All at once Iphegenia blazed with Clytemnestra's own passion. "*Heed me, Mother.* You must stay here. It will be better for us both. Let the old slave take me. I will not mind his tears. But do not you cry. I forbid you to shed tears!"

For one fierce moment Iphegenia's arms swept around her mother, holding her so tight that Clytemnestra's body would forever remember the imprint of that young living form. Then she had turned, was free, was walking down the path through the sweet grasses without looking back.

IX · SACRIFICE

THE OLD SLAVE escorted her, as she had wished, and he did weep. Through all the camp, a solemn silence was proclaimed. In the holy grove, Calchas somberly initiated the rites with the sacred baskets. The fires blazed with the meal-cakes of purification, and the water and the wine were poured. Agamemnon, his face a mask, circled the altar as was prescribed, from left to right. And a chant was raised, a chant for the daughter of the lions, who came to bring salvation and victory to all of Hellas.

Give me the bridal garlands to crown my hair. Bring me the purification of the blessed water. Weave the dance around the altar of Artemis the blessed. With my blood I shall wash away all stain and sin my people have committed against her sacred name.

Artemis was waiting for her. She felt her loving presence by the altar. Iphegenia turned to Agamemnon with those eyes so grave, so uncondemning, so early old.

"Father, I come here at your bidding and of my own free will.

53

My body I give to the gracious goddess, on behalf of our country, and of all of Hellas."

So she spoke, and a spell of astonishment fell over the encircling throng. Agamemnon heaved a sigh and turned his head aside and wept beneath the protecting cover of his robe.

Talthybius, whose charge this was, stood forth to proclaim reverent silence and attention.

Calchas the seer put into the gold-studded basket the sacrificial knife. He crowned with garlands Iphegenia's head.

Achilles circled the altar carrying the basket, sprinkling at the same time the lustral water. His voice was steady. "Child of Zeus, slayer of wild beasts, whirler of the gleaming moon, receive this sacrifice we offer, the undefiled blood of an untouched maid. Grant an untroubled voyage for our ships; grant that our spears may sack the towers of Troy."

The men whose duty it was to hold the sacrifice aloft stepped forth, their faces fixed. Then it was that Iphegenia's voice rang shrilly, a child's voice once more and filled with fear.

"Father, do not let them touch me! I will stand still for it. I will be quiet."

But Agamemnon, who had put fatherhood from him as kingly duty, brusquely bid someone step forth and bind her mouth with a gag. He could not believe that she would not cry out, with that ill omen putting another curse upon his house.

Men's hands lifted her, limp in her flowing dress, high above the altar. Men's hands held her there, outstretched and rigid, as they had so often held the sacrificial beasts. Men's hands tore at her girdle, cast her saffron silks to earth. And a deeper silence fell upon the watchers as they beheld her virgin beauty, which surpassed all visions in their dreams. And the glade rang with the silence, with the mute pleading in her eyes.

The goddess is here. The goddess is waiting for me. I must be brave.

The knife flashed downward, and the blood gushed forth.

As the blood of Iphegenia dripped upon the altar stone, a tremor stirred through the assembled host. Cold fingers touched their necks. A spellbound moment, and then the cry went up.

"The wind! The wind has risen!"

The shout of joy and triumph roared to the heavens. From the back fringes of the circle, men began to run. Soon all down the harbor sails began to bell. Swords were unsheathed and sharpened; armor glinted in the sun. Exultant voices sang the songs of war. Soon proud ships sailed to the east, their decks and riggings clustered thick with men who dreamed of glory and whose thoughts were all on Troy.

They left behind them on the deserted beach a dead girl for whom no funeral prayers were made, and a stony woman who presently, implacably, turned toward her home that was a home no more.

True to the lost daughter's bidding, she wore no inky garments and shed no tear. But she had disobeyed that other plea. Clytemnestra had seen. She had seen it all.

CLYTEMNESTRA

III

X · THE WATCHER AT THE GATE

IN THE RED CITY *on the mountaintop, Clytemnestra raged. Grief turned to anger; passion turned to hate. She walked the ramparts in the night and watched and waited. All Mycenae waited. And her passion and her torment grew.*

She had a lion heart, but in a female body, which the people of her time regarded with too light respect. She needed a man beside her—as queen, as woman.

She took her husband's cousin, Aegisthus, son of Thyestes, as her lover.

In the east, the proud-prowed ships swept like the sons of Caurus on Troy. Helen preened herself in the Orient sun. There were deeds of bravery, cowardice and folly. Cassandra, the virgin Trojan princess doomed to a gift of unbelieved prophecy, saw dark visions. Poets sang songs of arms and men. A siege began, a wooden horse of treachery was built, and topless towers burned.

Ten years passed.

Clytemnestra waited.

THERE IS A PLACE, high above the Lion Gate, where rust-red stones form platform and parapet. Where the sky, and the company of the gods, seems very near. Rocks, olive groves, desert and the road to the sea spread out below—a miniature world. Beyond lie mountains—bleak, awesome, threatening by day; lowering hulks by night; crowned here and there by the monolith shapes of other city-kingdoms. And beyond them yet, the sea; Poseidon's wine-dark, turbulent, ever-changing sea, across which one day—the gods and the fair winds willing—Agamemnon would come home.

The man stood, shivering slightly in the predawn chill. There was a pallet of straw for him, against hewn stone that provided a sort of shelter, but he preferred to stand. Or stride, bringing life back into limbs grown numb from waiting, not wanting to risk dropping off to a sleep that would mean certain death. He was the Watcher at the Gate, the security and the conscience of Atreus' city, charged with sounding the alarm of approaching danger, heralding coming joys. For twelve full months now he had had this duty, like a faithful dog outside his master's hut. The nightly conference of the stars were now his friends; he knew them all, their settings and their risings. He knew much more, too, which he kept in the careful counsel of his heart.

No dreams visited him, for sleep's enemy, fear, stood guard beside him. Now and again he sang, but never long. Music brought man's tears, for the words recalled past splendors and bygone honor, and he knew too well how the House of Atreus had changed from the days of old.

"May the gods be kind soon," he muttered underneath his breath. "May they grant release from trouble." Further than that he dared not breathe, not even to the gods.

He leaned his spear against the wall and turned to glance down at the three altars, each with its statue, that stood in the open court before the dromos. Zeus, god of gods; Apollo, author and giver of light; Hermes, mischief-maker and messenger. They know, he thought. They know all inmost things, even the queen's. And they, too, wait.

He was, in his own way, poet, and in the depths of his mind phrases began to turn that he dared not sing.

He spat three times, his lips hurriedly forming a primordial prayer. Odd how in the night a man could feel all at once as if his thoughts were read. The skin on his neck prickled, as though someone on cat feet had approached behind him. Impossible, since he stood against the wall. Yet in an instant his hand tightened around his spear, his body was alert and tensed; his weathered face swung back toward Eastern blackness.

A new star burned.

No, not a star. The beacon fire, on the farthest mountaintop near to the sea. The signal, long since prearranged, so long awaited.

Victory. Troy is taken.

Agamemnon comes.

One moment of stunned joy, almost disbelieving. And then the Watcher was running, running over the red stones. Crude stones rough-hewn for soldiers; majestic stone staircases polished by women's sandaled feet. Words pounded unspoken with his pounding heart. *I'll be the first to start the triumphal dance. The king comes, the rightful king, my master. I will once again hold in mine his dear hand which the gods have blessed.* For the rest, his tongue was silent. The house itself, if walls could speak, would tell its story to the returning king.

What he did cry as he ran was, "Awake the queen!"

CLYTEMNESTRA was not asleep. She had not slept, she sometimes thought, these whole ten years. Now she lay on the royal couch as she had done so often, staring at the ceiling with dry and burning eyes. In the corner, a small lamp cast its fitful shadows on the wall. She could not bear darkness, she could not bear solitude, for whenever she closed her eyes the pictures formed. *Iphegenia, bound upon the altar.*

Was that why she had opened herself to Aegisthus' lust? If so, the old narcotic no longer worked. He slept now, heavily, the once-firm body sated with wine and luxury. But if she tossed on their couch, as the sleepless will, he would reach for her. Her flesh recoiled from it. She slid cautiously, soundlessly, to her feet. The lamp spread its faint warmth over her bare body—still beautiful; the years had not bloated her as they had Aegisthus but rather pared and hardened, until she could herself be a statue carved in stone.

She had kept herself beautiful deliberately, so that returning Agamemnon should desire her—should know what it was to have one's arms ache for a living, beloved body one could no more enfold.

She reached for the embroidered purple cloak—Agamemnon's cloak, which in her chamber she, the true ruler of Mycenae, wore.

O gods, be kind! Deliver him back into this room, into my hands. For Iphegenia's sake, for my daughter's sake.

At that moment she heard the Watcher's voice.

"The queen! I must see the queen! She must rise from her bed like the dawn! Troy, Troy has fallen!"

The cry burst from her throat, springing from deep within her—the cry of triumph. Then, swiftly, she was spinning round, tearing off the forbidden cloak and pulling on the finest gown at hand. Not waiting for handmaids, ignoring Aegisthus' half-drunken stirrings. She knew, too well, the murmurs of the city. No one would say that Agamemnon's queen was not the first, the greatest rejoicer at his returning.

Now her little handmaidens were tumbling in, still sleep-webbed, excited, fearful of her displeasure. Beyond the crimson curtains at door and window, Clytemnestra could hear the echoes of her cry traveling from mouth to mouth. Messengers were hurrying beyond the palace enclosure through the city; beyond its walls, past hovels huddled at its base, to the outlying farms.

Attendants would be following in various directions, carrying oils and incense for sacrifice.

Troy has fallen. Our king is coming home.

Her hands fumbled, fastening the golden clasps at the shoulders of the breath-soft linen. The maids were girdling her with gold, circling her eyes with kohl as pomp demanded. They fluttered about her, twittering birds in a lion's path. Then she was free of them, moving like wind down the triumphal staircase, out into the courtyard. Fires blazed; below her down the hill lesser flames leaped everywhere at outdoor altars. Only a faint luminosity in the purple sky spoke as yet of dawn. But the air was fresh, free of the haunting fear that always like an enemy crept near, slunk away, recurred.

For so long the burden had galled her soul, sick with the evil that had been. Now the end was near.

She cast incense upon the palace altars and stood motionless, praying to Zeus.

Cry Sorrow, Sorrow, yet let good prevail. . . .

The day broke. The day so long awaited. . . . Up from the streets of the city, up from the small rooms that rimmed the lower level of the palace came the assembled elders. The king's counselors, those nobles and civil leaders who had been too aged to sail for Troy. For ten years they have crouched, Clytemnestra thought grimly, like crows awaiting carrion. They would have bloodied meat, and soon.

She sent word that she awaited them, that she had news. Back in her chambers she bathed, ordered the maidens to rub her with perfumed ointments, adorned herself in queenly robes. White, she thought, symbol of chastity; embroidered with gold to remind them I am doubly royal. The purple cloak of office, for the same shrewd reason.

"Why do you bother?" Aegisthus murmured, watching. "It

lowers your dignity to so honor them, as though you need their approval. That pack of old baboons! Why do they matter?"

Fool! She had known for some time that he was a fool. But I need him, Clytemnestra thought, wincing at the admission. He's weak; well, I knew that, too, didn't I? Only his weakness shall not subvert my strength. She made an angry gesture, sending the maids fleeing the chamber in trembling haste, then swung upon him.

"You are not yet king. And you are no diplomat, Aegisthus, remember that." Her eyes narrowed. "Dressed and pomaded and it's not midmorning? What are you up to?"

He came up behind her, sliding an arm about her waist, his voice silky. "You don't expect me to allow my queen to go out before that pack of curs alone?"

"*Oh, yes, I shall.* You are not my consort. This game is too deep for you. And dangerous. I warn you, don't try to meddle in state matters."

Their eyes locked. She had kept her voice a whisper, for the walls had ears, but its tone was unmistakable. It was Aegisthus' gaze that dropped.

"You should have been a man," he muttered. "By Hera, you're no true woman."

Yes, she should have been a man, she thought. If she had, everything would have been quite different.

She went out, striding like Aphrodite on delicate high-arched feet to face the assembled elders.

Baboons, Aegisthus had said. It was an apt metaphor. They stood, who would have looked more natural crouched, and their leader, oldest and most acid among them, plucked at his beard.

"We come obedient to your bidding, noble queen." The words rolled unctuously from his tongue, but did they veil a hidden threat? "With our king and leader absent, his throne unfilled, we owe our duty instead to his lady wife. We have observed the altar smoke, and we ask in love: Do these sacrifices rise for good news received?"

As if his ears had not already heard every flapping of the wings of Rumor. Clytemnestra's lips formed the requisite formal phrases smoothly. "As the proverb says, good news should be born with sunrise from the womb of night. But greater joy than you dared hope is yours. Our Argive men have captured Priam's city."

Ritual surprise, shaking the ranks with murmurs of disbelief: "Have what?" "We must have heard you wrong." "We can't believe it." "Lady, speak the message clearly."

A sudden impatience with this protracted formality swept through her. "Troy is ours. It fell last night. Is that clear enough for you to understand?"

"Happiness fills our eyes with tears at this news."

"They show your loyalty."

"But how can you know? What proof? Was it some dream you had, persuaded you?"

"Dream! You dare take me as one who would make public proclamation of such imaginings?" She had allowed her irritation to show; that was not wise. The old man drew himself up with dignity.

"Troy fell last night, and Troy is far away. Surely you feed yourself on unconfirmed report. A vision of some god? Some women do so. . . ."

"I am no ignorant girl!" She caught herself, went on smoothly. "A god indeed was the messenger. The god of fire!" She was filled all at once with an exhilaration, a triumph in revealing the success of what had been her planning.

"At Troy's fall, on Mount Ida a messenger first lit his signal flame. And from there, beacon flashed to beacon across the mountains of the world. On Hermes' crag in Lemnos; on the rock of Athos; crossing the Aegean like a whip of lightning, and the fish danced as at sunrise in the beacon's glow. Makistos, Euripus, Messapia, Cithaeron, Aegiphantus—everywhere, each night these ten years, I have had men watching. And the last, at neighboring Arachnaeus, flashed the news to Atreus' palace. A message, sent to Clytemnestra from Troy, of Agamemnon! Today the Greeks hold Troy!"

Today, in that conquered city, Helen would feel the wrath of the Greeks. Helen, for whose sake her sister's bed had been deserted, for whose rescue her sister's daughter had died. Helen the beautiful, who cared only for comfort, adulation, luxury. She was not in luxury now. . . . A faint cruel smile, born of a thousand childhood slights, curled Clytemnestra's lips. Almost she could see her, could hear rising from narrow smoke-filled streets the screams of the captured, mingled with the savage shouts of those who'd captured them. Women of Troy were prostrate over dead husbands, brothers; the old mourned dead sons and grandsons. *They* had bodies over which to grieve. She had not even that of Iphegenia. Iphegenia was gone. Because of Helen. Because of Troy. Because of Agamemnon.

Well, Troy was suffering now, and Helen with it. As for Agamemnon. . . . She pulled herself up tall, tall as a man. "Go to your homes. Make sacrifices there, as I have done. There yet remains our army's journey home. If in that captive town they reverence the gods, and profane not the holy places"—she fought down the image of the Grove of Artemis and Iphegenia —"they shall sail home free from the taint of sin, those whom no wakeful anger of the forgotten dead waits to surprise with vengeance. . . ."

Don't speak of that. She must not speak of that. She must herself remember the warning she had given to Aegisthus. She smiled, graciously, sending the elders on their way. The sun was hot. She needed coolness and privacy within the palace, needed to lay aside diadem and cloak, needed to plan.

THE WATCHER AT THE GATE 67

Hands like pincers plucked at her garments as she swept inside. Clytemnestra whirled, words of anger dying on her lips.

"Madam." The girl shrank back, almost treading on the pale boy who lurked behind. Spiritless children, Clytemnestra thought with the now-familiar irritation. She still thought of them, when she remembered them at all, as children. Yet Electra was near fourteen now, well to the age when she should be a wife. We must see to that, after everything else is settled, after Agamemnon's home. She was royal, after all; there must be someone who would marry her for dowry, despite the too-thin body and those eyes . . . why must she always look at me like that? The way Iphegenia must have looked at Agamemnon from the altar. . . .

"What is it?" she asked shortly.

Electra's voice was whisper, yet she went on bravely. "Madam, is it true? The king, my father, is coming home?"

"You think I would have lighted sacrificial fires on the strength of rumor?" Clytemnestra snapped. Then, seeing the child recoil, she bent and brushed back a lock of lank, dark hair. Poor mouse, it was not her fault she was so—forgettable. "You must take your brother and make your own prayers at the altar, for the righteous army's safe return."

"I shall pray for my father's safe return."

Why did Electra always look at her like that, with eyes too old, too grave, as though they saw too far? The boy's eyes had it too, at times, that look of immemorial sorrow. They were too young to have the memories she did of Iphegenia. Or of their father, either. Clytemnestra straightened, patted them absently, turned them toward the door. Then she took a deep breath and went, not towards her private rooms as she would have wished, but toward Aegisthus' chambers.

She had best tell Aegisthus what had taken place and soothe his ruffled feathers. The audience with the elders had been more

strain than she cared to acknowledge. All at once, despite the
heat, she felt a chill.

Dreams, the old men had said, implying she was mere
woman, given to the irrational that she so scorned.

She did not dream. She did not dare to dream.

XI · ROYAL WELCOME

DAYS WENT BY, days of waiting and of rumor, for the message of fire had traveled much faster than even the fairest wind could make ships fly. The high Mycenean air danced in the golden sun, and the minds and moods of men shifted endlessly, echoing.

The hand of Zeus had cast the proud of Troy from their high place, had dispersed the swollen wealth of that great kingdom. But to achieve this end, Hellas—both palace and hovel—had known searching sadness. War was a banker, with human flesh its gold. Men had died nobly—for another's wife. And so, from anticipated grief, sprang gall that fear must hide.

Ecstasy, which had leaped high with the altar fires, died with their embers. Troy had fallen. Clytemnestra said so. But no witness to that fact had yet arrived. Ought they to have believed, or had the news been only some inspired deceit? The fantasy of a child or of a woman?

Had the fires and the queen made fools of all Mycenae?

They wondered, in farms and narrow city streets, and the sun blazed hot, and the air hung still. In the red-walled halls of the House of Atreus, Clytemnestra waited. Aegisthus paced and

69

shuddered. Two forlorn children longed for their father's safe return.

And then, one morning, a herald crowned with olive leaves came striding across the long plain from the shore. Far off behind him followed a column of armed men, sheathed in hot dust. All Mycenae gathered on the ramparts as the news spread, kindling one great flame of hope.

Up the long sloping ramp the herald ran, to fall sobbing with joy before the Lion Gate.

"Argos! The red earth of my ancestors, after ten long years. I am home, home . . . the one hope that proved true." As the elders, by right of place, gathered close round him, the herald lifted his voice in prayer. "Now blessed be Argos, and the sun's sweet light, and Zeus and Apollo! Gods of the city, and Hermes god of messengers, hear my prayer! Bless the returning remnant and welcome with shining eyes the triumphant chieftain."

The murmur spread like the rising tide from the elders to the throng behind them. *Agamemnon. Agamemnon comes.*

The herald, rising, rubbed the tears from his face with the back of a sweaty arm. "He comes! Bringing light into darkness for every Argive citizen, so greet him royally." He reached gratefully for a cup of wine extended to him. "My thanks. These past ten years I've prayed for life; now I can die in peace."

"Longing for Argos tormented you?" a woman murmured gently, and he nodded. The mouth of the leader of the elders twisted.

"Your suffering has its happy side. We longed for you."

"You mean you missed us." The herald's eyes narrowed. "Or do you mean more?"

"Missed, and needed. Our hearts were dark with trouble."

"What trouble? An enemy? Threats in the king's absence?" He stopped, for the old man had suddenly grown still.

"Least said, soonest mended." The elder, like an old crow

folding wings, seemed to shrink into himself. The eyes were hooded.

There had been no sound, no signal that human ears could hear, but the crowd too stilled. From high above them on a palace terrace a voice rang out.

"I sang the joy of this victory long ago, when fire against a night sky told me that Troy was sacked and shattered. And you scolded me, chiding me as a foolish woman. Still I made sacrifice of thanks, and throughout the city the women celebrated with songs of praise in the temples. Now the king comes home, my honored husband! Fling wide the gates in welcome! Take to him this message: Let him come quickly, Argos longs for him, and the queen is waiting. He will find a wife as faithful as he left, a watcher at the gate, knowing one loyalty only, implacable to her enemies and in all ways unchanged. Of pleasure found in other men, I know no more than how to dip hot steel!"

By all the gods, that speech was absolute truth, Clytemnestra thought grimly, vanishing into the palace. Behind her she left a bewildered herald, a scandalized crowd and the ironic elders who knew full well the message behind the words. No matter. Her devious speech would be carried to the approaching Agamemnon, whetting his heart and lust. And beneath the surface guile she had spoken truly. She was unchanged from the stone woman who had seen her daughter die. And pleasure had naught to do with what she sought or found in Aegisthus' arms.

Let the city seethe with gossip for Agamemnon's ears. He would be, at the first, too busy to hear. Meanwhile, she had preparations to complete. During the days of waiting, she had thought long thoughts and woven a web of plans.

The sun burned, and the excited populace flew about, gathering olive branches to wave or weave as garlands. Women decked themselves for returning husbands. Girls who had been children when the army marched to sea brushed their dark hair, hoping to find lovers. The city hummed, fires blazed on altars, and the serpent of moving figures marched across the glittering plain. Stone and sand blazed white beneath the blazing sun.

Then they had come. The victorious returning warriors were there. Weathered, sun-blackened, wearing wounds and scars like signs of honor. Older; so changed by all that they had done and seen that watchers' eyes scanned and scanned again before the cries of recognition rose. And other cries, wrung from the hearts of men and women for the beloved faces that they did not see— sons, husbands, brothers, who would never come again. But there was no lack of recognition for the greatest of them all. As with one voice, the shout went up from a hundred throats.

"The king! Heir of Atreus! Conqueror of Troy!"

Snorting, the horses whirled the golden chariot past the ranks of soldiers up the entrance ramp. Behind, another chariot equal in splendor was piled with spoils of war. But all eyes were on that stalwart figure, bronzed until his skin glowed equal to his golden armor, the horsetail streaming from his kingly helmet and his jutting black beard faintly silvered. Beneath the heavy brows the black eyes blazed with pride. Agamemnon, greatest of all the Hellenes, had returned in triumph.

High above, hanging over a parapet as far as she dared risk being seen, Electra stared. Father. The king, my father. As splendid as I remembered; my lady mother was wrong to say I was too young. The eyes that used to fill me so with awe, that kindled with laughter sometimes when I danced before him. They're different now, as though they've looked on deepest darkness. Eyes like mine. Does my mother see that when she looks at me? Does he see me? Will I be a disappointment to him, too?

Her eyes fell on the figure standing motionless by Agamemnon's side. A strange woman. What was she doing in the royal chariot? An Eastern woman, Electra thought, an unfamiliar emotion twisting in her as she noted the high cheekbones and apricot-colored skin. The faintly slanted eyes gazed unseeingly off into the distance, and even in repose the slender body spoke of the grace of the gazelle. The thought flashed into Electra's head: She isn't here. Her body's here, but she herself is far away. That's why she's so still. I wish I could do that.

"Electra!" Orestes, thin and dark, hovered excitedly behind her. She had the advantage on him yet in height, though he was eleven now. "Is he here? Is my father here?"

"*Our* father." Electra felt a flash of superiority. The year-old boy whom Agamemnon had left behind had been too young to have even such slight memories of him as she cherished. Then compunction, and the fierce love she had always felt toward her brother, swept over her. "There he is. See, in the chariot! He *is* like a god!"

Orestes, peering forward, was caught back in the grip of a tall, quiet man. Aristocratic of bearing, he wore the short tunic and cropped hair of a slave. "Don't make spectacles of yourselves. Wait till you are summoned, so your father can welcome you with pride."

"Oh, Artcurus!" Orestes' tone was impatient, but there was affection in it. "It's my father. Don't you understand? That's my father!"

"Aye, I know, And you are Prince Orestes, and a prince must conduct himself as becomes a king's son, so the House of Atreus shall not be put to shame."

"To further shame, you mean," Electra muttered. She meant it to be beneath her breath, but the tutor's eyes fixed on her firmly.

"And you, miss, a princess too has standards that must be met. One of which is discretion. There are times for speech, and times for keeping silent—especially about things you cannot yet understand!"

Electra tossed her head. "I may be a virgin, but I am not a

fool. The queen my mother has been lying with my uncle these many years. You think I do not know the whole city laughs about her and that—that goat?" She meant to sound confident and scornful, but despite herself she shivered. She could not explain, or shake off, the strange coldness that possessed her whenever Aegisthus' gaze was on her or he brushed against her. She felt a faint fear now, as the tutor's voice cut in, so very quiet.

"It is not wise to think of these things, nor to speak of them, ever. There is to be a festival banquet, and you will be expected. Why have you not put on your court attire?"

"I have not got to it yet," Electra said in a small voice. A hot flush, starting deep within her, spread upward staining the olive skin. She would have died rather than admit the shame she felt, forced to appear thus appareled before the court, before Aegisthus, before her father. The women's court costume consisted of a flounced, tiered skirt of pleated linen, topped by a tight sleeved bodice, closely clasped beneath the bosom but baring that entirely in tribute to the mother goddess. It was a style magnificently becoming even now to Clytemnestra. I'm too thin, Electra thought miserably; my bones show, I've no breasts to speak of. *Like a withered grape,* Clytemnestra had flung at her once. *An old-woman child. Why can't you be like—* She had stopped short of uttering the never-spoken name.

But Father is home now. Father, who was always glad to see me. Who will remember me, Princess of Mycenae, now of age to wed. Perhaps he has brought one of the young heroes home to be my husband. When Iphegenia—

She never let herself think of Iphegenia.

Suddenly Electra was twisting like an eel out of her brother's and the tutor's reach. She was flinging herself through the nearest doorway, running down steep stairs, into the curtained darkness of her room.

The city-kingdom shimmered in the blazing heat. To Aga-

memnon, it equaled all the splendors of fallen Troy. The very
rocks of which it was built glittered like jewels with copper-rose
and silver, and among stones and dust the familiar green plants
of his childhood sprang up. He had come home—home to the
shade of olive groves, and the great throne room of the House
of Atreus, and Clytemnestra's chamber where translucent
scented curtains drifted in the lofty breeze. Not even the incense
of the burning Troy, not the taking of the Trojan princess, with
whom even Apollo had not had his way, could equal this.
Odysseus was right, he thought. We appreciate things more as
we grow older.

He *was* older. Ten years had marked him; it had marked
them all. But now that lay behind. Before was peace, and
honors, and the throne of his forefathers, and the adulation of
his people and his queen.

He prepared to respond graciously to the leading elder who
was greeting him with measured dignity, praise neither scant
nor fulsome. And letting me know, the old fox, that he'd
thought in going to war I'd sailed far from the course of wisdom. Only victory, and the spoils brought home, prompt him
to say the not-forgotten past's forgiven. And why the cryptic
comment: "Time and your own searching will reveal who has
been true, who false"? But time enough to seek into that tomorrow.

"My city, and her gods, receive from me the conqueror's
greeting on my safe return. For this, and for my just revenge on
Troy, heaven shares my glory." The phrases rolled like ripe
fruit from his tongue. "Your advice I note. We will set a day
for assembly and debate of affairs of state, and where disease
wants remedy, fire or the knife will purge the civil body for the
body's good. Now I would to my home, and my own altar-
hearth."

Eager figures sprang forward to assist him. Before one hand

was lain on the Lion Gate, there was a flourish of trumpets. The great doors swung wide. Agamemnon, about to step down, was arrested in mid-motion by the vision framed in the arch.

Clytemnestra. Clytemnestra, suddenly like a goddess in an altar niche. The gold-leafed diadem of the House of Atreus crowned her piled hair, her earrings danced in the light, the jewel wealth of her ancestresses dazzled on her proud bared bosom. Her eyes flashed, her voice rang out over the trumpets.

"Citizens of Argos! Before you, unashamed, I speak, a wife's love for her husband." And let them dare think different, her mind thought. "Time conquers modesty. I tell what I learned, untaught, of my own endurance, these ten long years of war. First, that a woman should sit alone at home without a man is a crying grief. Second is that rumors cannot be trusted, for if my king had died each time report repeated news of his death, his funeral pyres would have bridged the space twixt here and Troy. Many times despair noosed my throat. But now he is here—the springing torrents of my tears are dry. My happy heart welcomes my husband, the guardian of his home, our ship's firm anchor and the towering pillar that upholds this royal roof. Such praise is but his due."

In a swift gesture, like a bird spreading its wings, she knelt, prostrating herself in the dust beside the chariot. Then the proud head rose, the ringed arms reached forth.

"Dear my husband, step down from your chariot." Who was that woman? He had dared to bring home a concubine! "But set not on earth the foot that trod on Troy." She was younger by a good fifteen years. Her skin was still firm. "Servants, make haste, carpet his path with purple."

The maids were hurrying forward, spreading the ramp with the billowing crimson she herself had woven. Tyrian purple, the color sacred to the gods. Would Agamemnon remember and beware, or had his arrogance swelled so he would truly think this was his due? The woman seemed to gaze straight at her but

not see her. Those eyes. . . . Forget the woman. Let this insult
serve only to add fuel to righteous rage. She kept her voice like
honey, so he would not hear the true meaning of her words.
"Justice herself," Clytemnestra proclaimed carefully, "leads
Agamemnon to a home he never hoped to see."

Had she gone too far? Agamemnon frowned. "Daughter of
Leda, guardian of my house, your speech matches my absence;
both were over-long. Fit praise for a man should come from
other lips. Kneel not to me, nor woman me with soft attentions.
Your soft cloths invite the envy of the gods. It is dangerous for
a mortal to walk on such a carpet. I would be reverenced as a
man."

Did anyone but Electra, squeezing unnoticed through the
throng, truly see the look that flashed between man and wife?
For an instant, in her eyes, blackness veiled the sun and her
fingers tingled. The air crackled, as though swordsmen had been
suddenly engaged in a desperate contest she did not understand.

Clytemnestra's voice, like a shuttle, wove a spell. "There is a
sea that teems with purple dye, costly as silver, unceasingly re-
newed—a dark stream for the staining of fine stuffs. Who shall
exhaust the sea? This house, by the grace of heaven, has store
of crimson enough for one outpouring! You are no king of
beggary! Had oracles so spoken, I would dedicate twenty such
carpets for the trampling, to ensure safe journey's end for this
one life."

A wave of unreasoning panic washed through Electra. *Don't,
Father, don't! To walk on purple is to equate oneself with gods,
as did our ancestors when the curse first fell!*

As if he had caught the tenor of her prayers, Agamemnon's
voice became austere. "I have said how I can enter my palace
with an untroubled mind. I shall do nothing contrary to my
resolve."

"Tell me one thing. Would you never, in danger, have vowed
to the gods to do just what I now implore?"

"Only if an oracle had so prescribed."

Yes, he obeyed oracles; Clytemnestra knew that well. She threw all her will into remaining relaxed, remaining calm. Her voice wooed. "If Priam were conqueror, what would he have done?"

She had struck a responsive chord. Agamemnon laughed. "Walked on embroidered satin, I am quite sure."

"Why should you do less? Why do you humble your heart to the fear of censure from the populace?"

She had him. His smile spread. "Why, indeed? Yet the tongues of the common people speak with power."

"You are *un*common. Distinction bears hate as its price. To be unenvied is to be unenviable."

Father, hear me! Do not trust this woman! Electra flung the silent message wildly. Before her, the figures wavered and shimmered in the dazzling sun. It was as if they moved and spoke in a ritual dance.

Agamemnon: "It does not become a woman to be so combative."

Clytemnestra: "But it does suit greatness to accept defeat."

Again his laugh, tantalized, intrigued. "Why, here's a battle! What would you give to win?"

And her chuckle, deep and throaty, a tone she had not had these ten years. Not even with Aegisthus. "Yield! You are the victor of Troy. Give me too my victory!"

Eyes locking. Something in their gaze, the force of which Electra felt like a blow but could not understand. She reeled from it, her own eyes darting frantically, searching for release. The whole scene grew dark, grew bright; then the world righted itself, and she found herself looking straight at the strange woman in the chariot.

It was the most profound and unnerving moment of Electra's life. The woman had known her presence, had known *her,* and had come back from whatever dreamland she inhabited to tell her something. Help her? Warn her? Behind those slanting eyes Electra saw flames, saw blood. The Curse of the House of Atreus, at once past and future. And into it, like a knife of present reality, came Agamemnon's voice to his attendant.

"Come, kneel, untie my sandals. And may no envious god watch from afar. It offends modesty that unwashed feet should tread such costly treasure. But no matter. Troy's conqueror is conquered by Mycenae's queen. Treading on purple, I go into my house."

In the instant, Electra saw her father stepping down, all gold and bronze, onto that red-violet sea. She felt salt in her own dry mouth, the taste of fear. The feel of her fingernails digging deep into her own clenched palms. The scent of thyme in the rocks, and of men's sweat, and of the perfumed ointments on her mother's gleaming skin. The sound of her mother's long triumphant cry.

"Eleleleleu!"

It poured from Clytemnestra's throat, her head flung back as in a ritual exaltation. She was silhouetted, black against the blazing sun. Blackness closed in like the Furies, and Electra went down into it as into the cold womb of night.

XII · CASSANDRA

OW LONG she was unconscious, Electra did not know. She found herself sitting on one of the benches that lined the wall, leaning back against it. Her heart pounded, and there was pain in drawing breath. And she was cold, so cold.

No one had noticed, and for that she was so grateful. What shame to have disgraced the family by public fainting, and what rumor could have arisen from such display! It was quiet now. Much of the crowd had left, though some remained, and some of the elders. Her father and her mother had gone inside. The purple rug lay trampled in the dust.

The woman was still in the chariot. She simply stood, as animals dragged to the altar sometimes stood dumbly waiting. Her eyes no longer saw. Then the bronze-adorned doors of the palace swung open. There was a whisper of scent. Clytemnestra had returned.

"You, too, Cassandra, do you hear me? Get inside." She was speaking to the woman. A prickle of recognition ran down Electra's spine. Cassandra. All Greece knew the name: their tutor had spoken of it, weaving tales for herself and for Orestes.

Princess of Troy, and prophetess, she who had snubbed Apollo. Now she was here, gaunt and alien, elegant even in her travel dust. "You may thank Zeus, this palace bears you no ill-will. Agamemnon wishes you treated well. You shall stand by our altar and take part with all our household in the cleansing ritual."

There was no response. Clytemnestra's voice thinned.

"Be not so proud, woman. Even Heracles was once a slave. No one bears that yoke willingly, yet when misfortune falls there's no help for it. Our house, long-established, can be generous. You shall have all that is due your station, and more besides."

Silence.

"She needs an interpreter." The words came from Electra impulsively. She had not meant to betray her presence, but to her relief Clytemnestra only swept her a glance of faint distaste.

"Tell her with signs. I have no time to waste in argument. The victims for sacrifice wait at the central hearth. If she has wits about her, she will obey." Clytemnestra's imperious gaze flashed round. Then she swung back inside, the tap of her sandals growing faint along the corridors.

Cassandra's eyes closed. A wave of pity washed through Electra. Timidly, she plucked at the bedraggled pleated silk; gestured her to step down, enter; pantomimed prayer. The dark gaze, focusing on her with difficulty, softened. Cassandra obeyed. She walked stiffly, dazedly, following Electra's lead, through outer and inner porticoes with their painted pillars, up the slope of the west main passage to the towerlike court before the great west portal.

The sun dazzled on the ramparts, gilding the world spread out on either side—the Cyclopean walls; the Plain of Argos framed by Mount Tretos; Mount Parthenion; Artemision, the sacred mountain of Arcadia. The scene as always filled Electra with intoxicating pride. Truly we are the heirs to the gods, she thought, flashing a glance at her companion to see if she shared the wonder. But Cassandra responded to nothing, not even when they went within the palace proper and moved down the frescoed corridor to the main court. She had withdrawn into that inner world.

From the megaron, or main public building, came the sound of chanting and the scent of incense. They were about to begin the sacrifices, Electra thought; we shall be late. She did not want to miss a moment of the splendid rituals that would mark her father's safe return. She plucked at Cassandra's garment, more confidently now, and Cassandra shook herself faintly and responded. Then, just as Electra was hurrying ahead of her across the portico, she was stopped by a shrill cry.

"Eleleleleu!"

Cassandra had frozen like a statue, stricken. Her eyes, widened with horror, stared at the stone figure that stood behind the libation basin. A stream of words, in a weird tongue like swallows' twittering, poured from her rigid lips.

"Apollo! Yes, that is the Lord Apollo." Electra could recognize that single, oft-repeated phrase. She laid her hand reassuringly on Cassandra's arm, glanced at those who stood and those who served within the courtyard. "We worship the same gods, then. But come, the great altar is within, where you may pray to Zeus."

Cassandra jerked herself away. But Electra felt the woman knew nothing of where she was or whom she saw. This must be like the Delphic oracle. A woman in a world unseen. Fascinated, Electra watched as Cassandra tore at her hair, moved inexorably in ever-widening circles, and all the while the flow of that strange, hypnotizing voice went on.

For Electra, watching, the courtyard too began to whirl. The scent of incense and perfumes from the throne room grew stronger, mingled with the stench of smoke. The sacrifices had begun, but she could not move. Pictures flashed before her eyes

. . . all the long bloody story of the family curse. Thyestes' banquet, Clytemnestra's hatred, the sacrifice of her sister . . . shuddering, she saw them all.

Then the feverish voice changed to a low keening, and the pictures also changed. An alien city; lovely women and stalwart men; Helen the beautiful, the despoiler. Blood and fire. Cassandra was mourning Troy, the fallen, and for a moment Electra, shaken, mourned it with her.

Cassandra gazed up to the roof of the portico, recoiled with another cry, her arms shielding her eyes. Her face went grey. Suddenly, with a savage gesture, she ripped the priestess garlands from her neck, tore at her garments, flung down the small gold wand she carried. Her feet ground them ruthlessly, compulsively. And the tears ran down her hollow cheeks, making rivers of sorrow in the dust.

Electra did the only thing she could. She ran forward, weeping also, to wrap her arms around a figure so bereft.

Slowly, Cassandra's frenzy stilled. The distraught eyes focused on Electra and saw her, really saw her as they had before. One slender hand reached out to stroke the girl's tangled hair. Then something happened that Electra would never speak of, never would forget.

Cassandra knelt down on the painted floor, placed both her hands upon Electra's shoulders. The dark eyes flamed. In that moment, which was outside of time, all the vision within Cassandra's mind was transferred to the girl. She saw, as Cassandra had seen, blood-dripping Furies like a ghastly choir crouched on the roof of the House of Atreus. Saw figures, their faces blurred, and so unknown, moving inexorably in a so-familiar room. A woman bathing a man. A hunting net snaring a human victim from whose streaming wounds the Furies drank their fill. A bronze axe falling. A woman with a lion's head, paired with a wolf. Electra's brain whirled, and the pictures formed and reformed.

Cassandra's hands tightened on her shoulders. The alien face, so full of grief and horror, was transformed suddenly with urgency and pity. In those black eyes, new pictures formed. A young man, an exile and a wanderer, in the travel-worn garments of another kingdom. Mourning; kneeling at an altar; taking a mighty oath on a bronze dagger. Coming home to the House of Atreus as from a long journey.

The face was not blurred now. It was Orestes. Orestes not as at present, but as he would one day be. The visions faded. Cassandra rose. Folded the trembling girl to her with a tenderness like balm. The thin fingers rested for a moment on Electra's head. She was blessing Electra, forgiving her, absolving her from deeds as yet unknown. Like an old woman then, in a calm beyond anguish, Cassandra took the lead, moving through the portico, through the bronze doorway of the prodomos, the outer chamber. Then, at the purple curtain that hid the throne room, she gasped and fell back, clutching at her throat.

"It's all right. It is just the smell of sacrifice, and the Syrian perfumes sprinkled on the floor to scent the feast." Electra spoke soothingly, though her voice was whisper. Cassandra shook her head. For a moment she turned back, gazing through the open doorway at the now-slanting sun. Her hand gestured ritually; her lips formed what must be prayer. She seemed to grow more tall, more still. With no further acknowledgement nor sound, she moved away from Electra, through the inner doorway, and the purple curtains fell behind.

ELECTRA did not follow. She leaned against a frescoed wall as the odors and the chanting swelled. She should go in. Clytemnestra would be angry, if she noticed. Father might notice and think she did not rejoice at his return. She had wanted to be present, but she did no longer.

The sacrificial rite soared to its climax and the procession emerged in splendor, passed through the prodomos, portico and courtyard, there to dissolve. Cassandra was among them; she gave no flicker of recognition towards Electra. Nobles, elders, leading warriors, Aegisthus, bowed in obeisance to Agamemnon, who dismissed them graciously. His immediate attendants, with Clytemnestra and apparently Cassandra, would now escort him to the south passage to his private chambers where he would perform the ritual cleansing bath in the red chamber. The other ranking warriors would do likewise in the bath of the guest chamber across the courtyard. Afterwards, they would reassemble in the throne room, cleared by then of the stench of sacrifice, for the great feast.

"Electra! Where were you? You missed it all!" That was Orestes, eager, pulling at her arm. "Father let me say part of the prayers. I did it well, with hardly any coaching, and our father was pleased." He flashed a proud glance at the tutor, who confirmed it, smiling. "Electra, what's the matter with you? Are you sick?"

Electra shook her head. She needed to be alone, but it was hard to brush off the brother who seemed so like a son. Of no matter the fact there was but three years' difference in their ages. Clytemnestra ignored him; it was Electra and the tutor who had reared him. She smiled at him now, trying to shake off the dreams that webbed her.

"I shall be all right presently. It was just the sun."

Not even to Orestes could she speak of what had occurred.

She followed their lead across the court to a secluded bench. There she yielded herself to quiet and to shadow. Orestes chattered, the tutor's low, amused tones chided, figures of nobles and ladies gathering for the banquet moved across the court, but she scarcely knew.

It was absurd, irrational of her to have been so shaken. Absurd that she felt afraid. Father was home, Aegisthus was effacing himself, and all would once again be as it had before.

XIII · RETRIBUTION

THE INTERIOR of the palace was dark and cool, even on the hottest day. Translucent linen curtains drifted in the breeze that carried all the fragrances of the Argive plain. Along the walls of corridors to the private apartments, the frescoes glowed. To Agamemnon, tasting his hour of triumph, wanting his bath, his wife, soft robes against his weatherbeaten skin, it all was sweet. The old dog, remembering him, fawning at his side, nails clicking against the painted stucco floor. Clytemnestra not the implacable shrew he had left at Aulis, but mellowed, still beautiful behind the formal court *maquillage.* And the other woman, the strange Eastern tigress whose fires were banked so deep beneath the stone façade. It would amuse him to wake those fires against her will. But now the ritual cleansing bath, and the private prayers, then the great feast—old friends to rejoice with, old enemies to impress. He nodded carelessly to Aegisthus, that lily-livered cousin who had apparently appeared and proved useful in his absence, but who so clearly was no more a rival.

"We rejoice at your return, cousin. You shall find all that is due you ready." Aegisthus murmured the formal phrases, ushering Agamemnon into the royal bathing chamber with its red-painted floor.

Agamemnon flashed him a curt glance. *We,* indeed; either the royal plural or an insolent, familiar linking of himself with Clytemnestra—both were out of place. But he would deal with that tomorrow.

"The woman, too, shall bathe with us," he said easily. "She is of our household now, and royal, and she too has come from war."

"Ah, but you first, my lord. You are highest in honor and rank only under Zeus." With effort, Clytemnestra kept her voice warm and flattering. Her heart pounded. She jerked her head, and at the signal the attendants left.

Agamemnon frowned.

"We shall attend you—your wife, your closest cousin. It is our royal duty and our royal privilege." Clytemnestra went to a bench, lifted a heap of purple linen that lay upon it. "See, a new bathing robe, fitting to your state, made with my own hands in these ten years' waiting."

It was all gold-embroidered with scenes of their house's history. How cleverly she had made it, as Athene's own spiders weave webs to catch their prey.

Agamemnon, relaxing, began to unbuckle his armor, and she moved to help him. Aegisthus, obsequious, was by the door. Did Agamemnon hear the heavy bar, so carefully oiled, slide into the bronze rings that would hold it fast? He shot a wordless summons to the Eastern woman who stood quiet, waiting, and she stepped forward submissively. Was stopped by Clytemnestra. *No,* no Trojan Chryseis would serve him now; she would do this task herself, feeding her emotion on every contact with his familiar flesh.

He was stripped, vulnerable. The lamp on the floor cast flickering light and shadow across his body in the close, unwindowed room.

Aegisthus handed Clytemnestra the embroidered robe, and she wrapped it round the king. Aegisthus lifted the heavy jugs and began to pour perfumed waters into the lustral bath.

Agamemnon laughed. "My dear, you are better at embroidery than at designing. These folds contain me. I cannot lift my arms."

"Have you not lifted arms enough?" Clytemnestra's voice was silvery, but all at once there was danger in it. All at once all the Furies she had fed with her own heart welled up to overflow in a cascading, triumphant laugh. "Arms on behalf of lascivious, unfaithful Helen. Arms against your own daughter, my child, my darling. Arms to embrace every Trojan harlot. The curse has come to full fruit, son of Atreus. Did you really think you would escape?"

She reached between her breasts to grasp the bronze ornament that separated them, and pulled it free—a knife, the sharp blade of which had been hidden beneath the clasps of her tight bodice.

The light flickered. Aegisthus grasped the handle of an axe, his back against the chamber door, braced and waiting. Agamemnon's eyes were wide, stripped of illusion and pride, at last comprehending. He fumbled frantically within the voluminous robe that was a trap, trying unsuccessfully to free his arms. His mouth opened, a red well of terror.

"Help! *Help!*"

Clytemnestra's arm rose. The dagger flashed. It was on Cassandra that it descended. Cassandra, who stood mute, knowing all, fearing nothing, hoping nothing. She fell against Agamemnon, her blood spurting out. Instinctively his arms within the great cloak caught and held her, half to protect her, though she was past protecting, half to shield himself. Cassandra's lips moved; the sound of the alien tongue emerged faintly like the song of a dying swan, and then was still. Aegisthus' axe swung up, but Clytemnestra's hand was swifter.

"*This* for my daughter, doomed Iphegenia. It is fitting you die as she in ritual prayer, you butcher. Did you think any bath could wash you free of her virgin blood?"

Agamemnon, retching, crying out in agony, recoiled.

"Help! I am wounded, murdered!"

No one near enough to hear would dare to enter, even could they have broken down the heavy door. The knife swung again. "And *this* for the tears I, Clytemnestra, shed over every harlot that held you in her arms!"

Groans of agony. "Murder—a second mortal blow!" Lamp flame casting weird shadows on the frescoed walls. The room a scene of carnage. Blood running in crimson rivers toward the drain in the red-painted floor. Did Aegisthus wield his axe? Afterwards he was to say he did, but Clytemnestra never knew. The blood spattered her arms, bare breasts, the pleated linen skirt.

"And *this* for Zeus the avenger! Praise and honor to him for he has answered all my prayers!"

Agamemnon fell. Backwards, belching forth his life with cough and retch, and from his mouth there spurted bloody foam, and then he was still. Clytemnestra's head went back and her laugh rang out, rang and rang until Aegisthus grabbed her by the shoulders and shook her roughly, and the knife dropped from her grasp.

"It is over. *Over!* Time enough for gloating when we are safe!"

She turned on him a glance of utter scorn. "Are you afraid? *Before* was time for that! Unbar the door, fling it wide, and leave all to me!"

Beyond the door there were running feet and voices crying out and hammering fists. The sounds, the panic, the danger were to her only as the roaring of the distant sea. At her terse word Aegisthus, his face pasty, pulled free the door bar. The door swung in upon them. The crowd in the corridor surged forward, then fell back.

Framed in the doorway Clytemnestra stood, the blood, like jewels, glistening on her skin. She was queen, and before that imperious authority the courtiers, even the guard, could but do her bidding.

"Bring a litter and bear this carrion to the central court. Then summon the populace and priests, and we shall make public answer to all your questions."

None dared disobey. The procession made its solemn way through the gallery of the curtain frescoes, through the south corridor, round past the guest chambers and into the court of the megaron. Women wailed and tore their hair, men beat their breasts, but Clytemnestra stood upright, following the corpses, with Aegisthus close behind her, and her eyes were dry. There on the square-painted plaster floor they laid the corpses down. Courtiers, attendants, dignitaries formed a still circle round them.

Agamemnon lay as he had fallen, on his back, webbed in the robe of treachery, and the embroidery glittered in the sinking sun. Cassandra, the prophetess whom none had heeded, lay across him, and from the portico the statue of Apollo gazed upon them with all-knowing eyes.

No one paid heed to the trio frozen on the secluded bench: The tutor, his hand across Orestes' mouth. The boy, suddenly so terribly young and vulnerable to be the dead king's heir. The girl, clutching tightly at his arm, life and blood seeming drained from her body. She stood and saw, and time whirled crazily because in the vision she had seen it all before.

Over the bodies, Clytemnestra spoke.

"I said, not long since, many things that were most seemly for the time. All of them, the time now past, I, without shame, unsay. How else, when one prepares death for an enemy most close, most dear, to lure him to rightous judgment save through a trap? For ten years, and for great cause, I planned this moment. At last, the battle was struck, and victory mine. This is my work; I claim it. So stands the case, elders of our city. You may take it as you will. The wine of wickedness this man stored in this house, he now has drunk down to the dregs."

Silence. Men glanced one to the other, each wanting another to break the silence first. The oldest elder, tottering like a wizened vulture, stepped forth at last.

"The brutal effrontery of your words robs us of speech. *Seemly,* you say. Is it thus to boast so shamelessly over a husband's corpse?"

His words set a tone, casting this as private and domestic crime. Clytemnestra's eyes sharpened. "Think me not some stupid woman; my pulse beats firm. Approve or censure; to me it matters not. I speak what you all know. Here lies my husband, Agamemnon, dead. His death is justice. Any who dare threaten me with vengeance should have offered him the same when he sacrificed his child. Iphegenia, born of my travail, he sacrificed for a charm, for a wind to Troy! And none of you rose to stop him; you pushed him on!"

"It was the will of Artemis." The murmur came uneasily from the rear. Clytemnestra swung around.

"Aye, because some gross brute of you took the life of her loved deer! Agamemnon, king of kings, must betray private loyalties for the public good. And he did—through pride, through dreams of glory! He has his glory now."

"For wife to turn on husband . . . that most sacred bond—"

"What of the bond of blood between parent and child? Is that as nothing?" Clytemnestra's breasts rose. Never had she been more beautiful, more implacable, as she turned to face the statues of the gods and the great hearth. "You gods, you Furies who haunt this house, you citizens of Argos, hear the oath I swear! Clytemnestra was Agamemnon's wife; henceforth her name from his be freed! Dressed in her form, a phantom of vengence, a ghost of Atreus poured forth this blood in payment of old crimes. By Justice, guardian of my slain daughter, and by her avenging Fury, I proclaim I have no cause to fear."

Her arm stretched out, and Aegisthus, until then half-hidden, came through the crowd that parted. Clytemnestra turned toward him a brittle, dangerous smile.

"No human avenger's tread shall shake this house while my staunch kinsman, rightful heir to the Lion Throne, kindles upon my hearth the ancestral fire. Now to the powers that persecute our race, I offer this sworn pact: The sinner has died. Blood has been shed for blood. With this deed now *I* am content; let them be also and depart this house. The debt of the House of Atreus is paid."

She stepped back. A murmur traveled through the crowd, quickly hushed as Aegisthus cleared his throat.

"Oh happy day when Justice comes into her own!" Was his tone too unctuous? He had good cause for sincerity, men reluctantly agreed, recalling Thyestes' grisly banquet. "I planned this killing, as was just; I plotted this whole evil snare and caught my man. I can die now satisfied."

He did not see, as the crowd did, the incredulous anger that flared in Clytemnestra's eyes. The leading elder's voice was dry. "You may have your wish. Since you claim you alone laid the whole plot, justice demands that Argive hands will stone you dead."

Aegisthus bristled. "Is this how the servant lectures from the lower deck the master on the bridge? You shall learn, though old, how harsh a thing is discipline when age does not bring wisdom. Chains and hunger are great medicine to school the mind."

The old man's eyes never flickered. "You woman," he said softly. "When Agamemnon went to fight, you stayed at home— to lie on silken cushions and seduce his wife. Think you we believe that against a general of generals, *you* could scheme a murder?"

"Do you dare offer insult and treason to your rightful king?" Aegisthus' voice snapped. "Guards! Pull forth your swords!"

The old voice, like a knife-edge, replied: "Our swords too are ready. And our honor. We can die."

" 'Die!' We accept the omen. Fortune hold the stakes!" Aegisthus' grip tightened around the handle of the axe that he still carried. A current ran through the circle; men's hands sought weapons.

"*No!*" Clytemnestra cried. "No more violence! There has been enough of death! We'll all reap grief enough; let us not plunge deeper into blood. Elders, I beg of you, yield to destiny and go home before you come to harm. What we have done was fore-ordained. Go now, in silence, and each by your own choice rejoice or mourn. I felled Agamemnon; I shall earth his bones. No funeral procession shall lay him in vaults of stone and iron. No, as is fit, his daughter shall meet him in the Underworld with her gagged and silent tongue. Leave him to Hades, and to the Furies who now, we pray to Zeus, have drunk their fill. Here in this city, we the last of the heirs of Atreus shall rule until my son Orestes comes of age."

The power of her presence, as much as reason or prudence, worked its spell. Slowly the crowd began to drain away as the blood had drained out of the slaughtered bodies. Aegisthus turned to Clytemnestra petulantly.

"Shall these gross-tongued men be free to offer insults? It is not fitting—"

"Hush!" Clytemnestra snapped savagely. Her head was aching intolerably. The weight of the jewels upon it was like a vise. I ought to feel free, she thought. The burden of the impotent years has rolled away. The single purpose to which all my energies have been directed is fulfilled. Where now is the ecstasy, where the triumph? I am only . . . empty. She turned, not waiting for Aegisthus, and walked away. Presently, he followed.

The two bodies lay, deserted, in the shafts of the setting sun.

In the shadows of the corner, the small immobile figures returned to life. The tutor, his arm stiff, took away his hand.

"My father," Orestes' voice said, small and wondering. "Electra, *why?*"

"Shh!" The hiss came from Electra almost without volition. As if by instinct she snatched up a cloak someone had dropped, wrapped it around them both, hurrying Orestes through a side corridor with the tutor close behind. She pulled them into a storeroom used only by the steward. "We're safe here. You must go away at once. Go quickly." At Orestes' bewildered protest, she turned frantically to the tutor. "You *will* take him? You must go by stealth, by the north stairway, and let none recognize you. Go to Strophius, king of Phocis, he was my father's friend. Orestes will be safe there, for he is not here."

She saw clearly now what it was that Cassandra had revealed. The figures whose faces had been blurred in visions, now were clear. Cassandra had foreseen the whole web of treachery, her own death and Agamemnon's, and had tried to prepare Electra and to warn her. Had foreseen, too, what Electra's instinct and reason both proclaimed: that Orestes' life was at stake while he was in Argos. He, yet too young to rule, was Agamemnon's son; he was a rallying-point for all those who would in time rise up against Clytemnestra and Aegisthus. Electra was uncertain whether time would prove or disprove Clytemnestra's vow that revenge was ended. Bond between parent and child outweighed for her that between wife and husband. But all maternal love had been stored up jealously for Iphegenia, and whether she would suffer her other children's blood to be shed could not be seen. But about Aegisthus, Electra had no illusions. Aegisthus, her uncle, wanted his throne, his security, his queen; he would do anything to keep them safe.

He won't be afraid of *me,* she thought with dark contempt. No one thinks of me or notices me. And so I must stay here, however high the price. Must stay and watch, until the time is ripe.

The thought sustained her as she ran like a wraith through the back corridors, ferreting out wine and bread, wrapping them in a bundle. When darkness fell, she crept out through a hole in the wall no one else knew of, to meet Orestes and the tutor in a deserted shack, hard by the mountain's back.

She thrust the bundle at them. "Here. There's gold, too. I stole it from Aegisthus' room." The tutor's eyes filled with alarm, and she shook her head. *"He* won't find out. He's with *her.* There's food for a day's journey, and you can buy more. You'll be safe once you reach Phocis, only you must hurry." In a torment of loneliness, she clutched Orestes to her tightly.

"Go in peace. I love you. Don't forget that, ever! See, here in the bundle, there's a new garment that I wove for you. It will remind you. Now I must go."

Orestes' anxious words pulled at her as she turned toward the door. "Electra, don't go back! Come with us!"

She shook her head, forcing her voice to be calm and reassuring. "I must. It will be all right. I *know,* Orestes."

For she did know—the secret that she did not tell the frightened child, that she clutched to her heart during the hard climb to the acropolis and through all the much harder days that followed.

There had been one more vision Cassandra had revealed. Clytemnestra was wrong in thinking there had been an end to vengeance. Vengeance was coming on *her,* for Orestes would return.

ELECTRA

IV

XIV · EXILE'S RETURN

THERE WERE *other deaths. Whenever murder's done, a ruler overthrown, there are those who see, hear, think or feel too much. And those who, pitiably, just happen to be present.*

There were rumors. Whispers in the hot wind that Aegisthus did not wish any of Agamemnon's seed to live. That this was why, suddenly, Orestes was seen no more. The whispers were guarded, for Aegisthus had had himself proclaimed the king; he was truly wed at last to Clytemnestra, he sat upon the Lion Throne; there was danger in breathing anything against him.

On that day when the sky rained blood, the two refugees had tried to flee unnoticed. But where royal blood is concerned, even the walls have eyes. A shepherd seeking a wandering sheep, a woman drawing water . . . but Orestes was the young lord, heir to Agamemnon, and he was beloved. So slowly, other rumors grew that would protect him. Orestes, that dread day had run away . . . the tutor in blind fear had kidnapped him . . . both of them, in the wilderness, had perished.

THERE HAD BEEN *a wedding and a coronation. But for Agamemnon, no funeral pomp and reverent rites. No procession of women beat their breasts and tore their hair; no prayers were said and no libations poured. No stone circle formed his grave, after the custom of the royal house. A flint-hearted widow and her paramour buried him in secret. He lay beneath a mound of earth outside the gate, and none dared weep for him where spies could see.*

If Electra his daughter mourned, she mourned in private. As she had learned, so young, to live unloved, now she learned the self-preserving caution of the slave. Despised, unwanted, shoved aside and shunned like an ulcerous dog, she grew into young womanhood thin and silent. All the passion, hate, loyalty of her heritage burned in her eyes.

THE TIDES *and the seasons turned beneath the blazing sun, and by the eighth year of Aegisthus' kingship, Mycenae on its mountaintop was like a citadel of bleached bones.*

CLYTEMNESTRA'S LIMBS ached, lying on the soft cushions of her golden couch. A lamp burned fitfully in the corner, for she could not bear the dark. She was alone. Aegisthus, who slept the sleep of the drugged when once he drifted off, could not tolerate that light. He needed the blackness of oblivion, whereas for her that pit of night was filled with writhing shadows and twisting forms. We're growing old, she thought. The breasts exposed by ceremonial costume were still firm, but she had that morning seen with shock the slackening of neck muscles, the crepey flabbiness of underarm. And had struck, with an oath, the small maidservant who had been watching her with pitying eyes.

My temper's growing short, too, she thought. I used to have control. And Aegisthus . . . she shuddered away from contemplation of the dissolute sagging of the eyes, the paunchiness of belly. Aegisthus, who had at last received all his heart's desires—revenge, adulation, fear, queen and crown—and who was still only an imperial clown.

Clytemnestra stirred uneasily, thrusting the cushions vainly in an effort to find the comfort that eluded her. With age, with his position on the throne secured, Aegisthus's wants had grown more simple and more profound. He wanted children, and she could give him none. He who had sated his appetites with lust now wanted to be loved, and she could not give him that, either. The capacity for human warmth had been burned out of her with Iphegenia's death.

She, Clytemnestra, was old enough to be a grandmother. But she would never deck the bridal bed of that beloved older daughter. Orestes, that son in Agamemnon's image, was gone, the gods alone knew where. And as for Electra. . . .

There it was again, the flash of nameless fear that washed over her whenever she remembered the overlooked younger girl. And she thought of her more and more of late. Electra at twenty-two, worn and gaunt, could have been taken for a peasant woman of middle age. A disgrace that she should thus make her mother seem even older. A disgrace, too, that she was still unwed.

That was it, the cause of this icy fear. Electra, the last offspring of the House of Atreus. Electra, whom Aegisthus had been curiously unwilling to have wed. Who could raise up a child that would avenge a kinsman's murder, as Aegisthus had avenged Thyestes' cannibal feast.

Aegisthus wanted a child, an heir. A child by Electra, conceived of his own seed, would at once assure the succession and be the only heir of Atreus who would be no threat. . . .

She must not let herself think along these paths.

Clytemnestra clapped her hands sharply, and the maid she had struck earlier appeared, rubbing sleep from frightened eyes.

"Bring wine," Clytemnestra ordered brusquely. "You need not look at me that way. I will not hurt you." The girl, even more terrified, obeyed, flinching as Clytemnestra flung up a hand to prevent her adding water to the dark brew.

Clytemnestra's own hand was shaking as she ordered the girl to leave. *I must control this. A queen must never be seen as weak. But I must sleep, or there is no control. Sleep.*

She went to her locked cupboard, took out herbs, which she sprinkled in the cup, a task she would entrust to no one else. Sleep from which there was no waking could come too easily.

Sometimes, she almost did not care.

But not yet, she thought. *No, not yet. I am still young; the mirror lies. I still have more to do. If only I could have one night's restful sleep.*

She lay herself down again, and her heavy eyelids shut out the shadows flickering on the wall.

ON THE ROOF, the soldiers stood their guard. The servants slept. Through all the House of Atreus no figure stirred.

"*Aiaiaiaiai!*"

The cry reverberated off stone walls through the corridors of the midnight house. Terror-filled forms sprang up; hair stood stiff with fear. Electra, on her narrow pallet, flung herself bolt upright.

"*What is that?*"

A bent form hurried to her side and held her tightly. The old nurse, now nearly senile, who was the only servant allotted her. "Madam, it is your mother."

"What's wrong?"

"Shh, keep away." The bony arms rocked her, the sharp whisper was pitched low. "I know that tone, which warns in dreams. That groan speaks like Fate. Whatever is happening, lamb, be wise. Keep away."

Footsteps running down the corridor. The curtain pulled open. Clytemnestra's little slave, the frightened one, tumbling in. "Madam, her majesty your mother bids you come at once!"

A fierce something she could not yet name flared in Electra's heart. Already she was flinging a cloak around her, thrusting off the old woman who would hold her back. "What is it?"

"We are to go pour libations on the king your father's grave."

"*You lie!*"

The words burst from Electra involuntarily. She had no knowledge of so doing, yet she grasped the maid's arms in her hands, shaking her as a dog shakes a rat.

"Madam, by the gods! We are to go at once, and you to lead us. Her majesty has dreamed a dream!"

"Aye, I warrant," the nurse muttered. She stumped to Electra, pulled her free. "Come, lamb, your eight years' longing will be fulfilled, even though at *her* bidding."

Throughout the palace, lamps sprang to life. Feet pounded over stones. As the gray light that presages dawn broke over the mountains, a procession wound its way down the long road toward the Lion Gate.

Clytemnestra was not among them. She stood at her window, watching with dry and burning eyes. Aegisthus will be angry. Aegisthus will say I was a fool, and worse. Let him. I ruled here first. I was truly fool when I thought I could ignore the dead. His blood cries out, as Iphegenia's did to me. I don't want to do this ritual; I don't believe in ritual; yet something in me forces me to do it. Otherwise I shall have no sleep forevermore. Lords of the Underworld, accept the gifts I send.

The dream still vividly possessed her. She had lain in childbirth travail, and had delivered—not the son Aegisthus longed for, but a snake. She had wrapped it in shawls and lulled it at her breast like a little child. And its loathsome fang had fastened on her nipple, drawing out clots of blood. Drawing her blood. . . .

DOWN THE LONG RAMP to the Lion Gate the procession wound. Figures silhouetted against a smoke-dark sky; slave women in long black cloaks, like a snake slowly creeping. Stillness. The faint predawn breeze touching cold fingers against the pallid cheeks. Dry cheeks, Electra thought dully. We have no tears left. Mournful, solemn tread. Offerings for the dead. Offered by slaves. I am a slave, too. Slave to the past. Slave to Aegisthus. My mother lets him have his will, that I, a princess, be shunted to one side, unwed, dishonored. Yet I know it is not only that he fears the threat I represent, being Agamemnon's seed. I know the story of Thyestes and Pelopia. And now, I am so tired I almost do not care. I am all burned out. It would be so much easier to die. But *someone* must remain alive who remembers the old days, and Agamemnon. Who will see that Agamemnon is avenged.

I am all that is left.

Electra shuddered, feeling the cold beat through the rough cloth of her mourning garments. She was twenty-two, she looked forty, and she knew it. She had grown dry and atrophied, while Clytemnestra with the years had burgeoned, like a flower whose petals grew brighter and more perfumed just before they fell. What did it matter?

They passed the grave circle of earlier Mycenean rulers, and a sleepy guard threw open the great gate. Agamemnon lay in no such splendor, nor in a beehive tomb such as should be his by right. His grave, unnoticeable beyond the Cyclopean wall, was a mere mound of earth. And now, these eight years late, Clytemnestra sent propitiations to the dead—because she dreamed a dream!

The women set down their burdens, the jugs and amphoras of wine and oil, beside the mound. So small, so pitiable in this barren plain, to mark a man so great! But what rite could possibly sanctify the ground where such blood was so spilt?

Electra turned toward the waiting women, the black veil dropping from her disordered hair. "You who both serve and order our royal house, since you have come with me, tell me what to do." Unexpectedly, tears welled in the eyes that had been dry so long. Her voice choked. "What shall I say, 'Father, I bring gifts from your wife, my mother, in pledge of mutual love'? How can I bless this holy oil? How can I speak those words, 'Send your blessings on those who sent it'? Do I pray in hypocrisy, or do I throw this drink to the thirsty ground, as dishonored as his blood that flowed, and go in silence?"

The women shifted uneasily, looked at one another. The wind blew.

"Help me!" The words burst from Electra. "Speak! Without fear of—those we fear, for our fate is known to the gods, and there is no escape for either you or me."

Again the stillness. Then a woman moved forward. It was the nurse. The old eyes, gazing on Electra, were filled with pity.

"Pray, as you pour the wine, for those who are loyal. Pray for yourself, and for one who has been long gone from the Lion Gate. And pray for all murderers, that the justice of god or man shall find them out. Pray simply, 'Let one come to shed blood for blood.' "

She means Orestes, Electra thought. Or is it I myself who should have taken action. Have I hidden behind my weakness and my womanhood? Why have I not long since sunk a knife into my mother's heart? Is it only because I fear the retribution of the gods? But the gods command that a king and father's life should be avenged.

My head hurts. I must not think like this again.

She picked up the libation jug.

"Hermes, herald and mediator, guide of the Underworld, bid the powers of deep earth receive my prayers! Now for the dead I pour water of purification and call his spirit: Father! Take pity on me Electra and on Orestes, your own son."

The words of the ritual, the words of her own heart, joined together and began to pour like water through a dam that has at last been broken down. "We are homeless, the price paid by our mother for Aegisthus. I live like a slave, and he in exile, disinherited, and *they* glitter in the wealth you won." Her breath caught, snatching back the bitterness that had begun to taint her prayer. "Give me clean hands and a pure heart, and ways unlike my mother's. Let those who killed taste death for death, but justly! My curse I stake to match their curse." Her voice blazed, then quieted. "Unto us, be gracious. We ask this blessing in the name of the gods, and of the earth, and of the victory of right."

The water, wine and oil were poured. Their bodies moved through the ceremonial patterns, the beating of the heads and breasts. The age-old words were repetitively intoned.

> *Let tears toll for the dead,*
> *Waste for waste and loss for loss. . . .*
> *Avert the evil day,*
> *Hold curse of blood at bay. . . .*
> *Hear from bewildered hearts our cry.*
> *Let tears toll for the dead.*

The ritual, so long delayed, was over. There was that vacuum of self-conscious silence that follows all such things. The women stirred, wrapping themselves against the blowing dust.

"Go back. The sky is lighter now. I would sit awhile alone." Electra dropped down on a rock. In twos and threes, hesitant, the women went. Hands touched her, rubbing the taut muscles. The old nurse. Electra leaned back.

"Cilissa, what is wrong? I've waited so long to do this ritual. And now I feel nothing. I am all burnt out."

"Things too long brooded on never turn out as we expect."

"What would you have me do, forget? Like my mother?"

"She sent the funeral gifts, after all."

"Yes. I wonder why. And why do I *resent* it, when I wanted it for him so long?" Electra shook her head.

The old hands massaged her temples. "You're getting your mother's headaches—"

"Don't *ever* say that! Don't compare—" She checked the irrational fury, reached out blindly. "I'm sorry. I don't mean to shout at *you*." If her head just did not hurt so; if her eyes would focus. . . . It was lighter now. The rim of mountains; the grey-pale sky; plain, groves and fields as bleached and colorless as life. The mound, with its wet stain of wine, its pitiful wreath. So little to adorn. . . .

That was *not* all. Something else was there, an alien thing she had not seen in predawn darkness. A lock of hair.

A lock of hair, laid on the tomb as one close to the dead would lay it. Hair newly cut, which had not been there before— she knew. Not a day went by that she did not scan this barren place, as she scanned the ring of mountains, watching, waiting.

"Cilissa, *look!*" Electra whirled with it, her eyes blazing.

"I see it. Hair."

"Not just hair! Color, form, texture, like my family's, like my own!"

"Your mother owed this duty."

"*She* would not. I dared not. But some one did—send this as an offering—to our father."

A flicker of fear throbbed suddenly in the old woman's face.

"*Say* it! Why must we be afraid? Orestes lives! Orestes has been here."

"Or sent it, because he dared not tread this earth."

"What does that matter? What does anything matter? Orestes is alive." Suddenly, impulsively, she caught the old woman to her. "Go inside," she said gently. "I want to be alone. To think. To pray. Go. It will be all right."

Then Electra was alone on the mountainside, the lock of hair in her hand, and the wind stung her face with the reality of dreams coming true.

Orestes is alive. Orestes sent this. He will come. The surge of feeling that swelled, overwhelming her, was more than she could bear.

She heard no sound; the Earth was silent. She saw nothing, for her vision was inward turned. Yet with the passing of time she knew she was not alone. She looked up, slowly, and a stranger stood on either side of her; but she was not afraid.

They were tall, strong, sun-bronzed, and at the sight of them something in her died a little. That picture she had cherished—a boy slight, vulnerable. Orestes, whom she had loved. Neither of these was he, they never could be he. Yet one was speaking, and emotion shook him.

"Know, henceforth, that when you pray, the gods hear and answer."

She recoiled like an animal trapped and wary. They had heard her prayers. And her prayers, however cautiously veiled, had been treason. She wet dry lips. "Do you know my secrets? What do you think was in my heart?"

"The name that has been there these many years. As yours has been in mine." His voice broke. "Electra, don't you know me? *Look* at me!"

She shut her eyes tightly against the blaze of hope. "You mock me. You are setting a trap to snare me."

"If I am," the young man said grimly, "I also trap myself." She could not respond. Faintly she heard the voice, turned away. "Pylades, where is that . . . oh, here." Cloth was thrust into her hands. "Don't you know this? Woven on your own loom, by you embroidered."

It was rough beneath her fingers, as her childish handiwork had been rough. The garment she had pressed on Orestes in his leaving, that he might have a talisman in exile, embroidered with a hunting scene because small boys loved hunting . . . she could not trust her credulous fingers, her eager heart.

She opened her eyes, and as though some omen spoke to her,

her vision fell not on the woven stuff but on the ground. On dusty earth that bore the mark of footprints. The procession had circled the grave, but had not dared come near it. Only two sets of prints had done so. Her own—and another's, from the opposite direction, approaching where the lock of hair had lain but where she had not stood. Yet their form and proportions, their heels and toes clearly outlined, were like as a mirror-image to her own.

"Orestes." The name came in a dry whisper, not a cry. She rose, stiffly. Then brother and sister were locked in a still embrace, their emotions too turbulent and deep for words.

"Pylades, come." Orestes, standing apart at last, reached his hand out to his companion. "Electra, welcome one who has above all men been my faithful comrade. He alone has been true friend to me in exile. We have come, straight from the Delphic oracle, and no one knows that we are here."

A question was asked and answered without words, and Electra knew her prayers indeed had brought reply. In instinctive accord, brother and sister turned to face the sun.

"Zeus, Zeus, behold us and the deed we undertake." Orestes' voice, so much quieter and older than she had expected, began the sacred covenant. And so much *one* they were that they had had no need to discuss or to confer. "Behold the eagle's brood bereaved, the eagle killed in the net of death, a viper's coils. Look on us, Electra, Orestes; orphans and exiles."

How vulnerable they were, young and defenseless, against the might of Mycenae's king and queen.

"The voice of Apollo drives me to dare this peril.

'Shed blood for blood, face set like flint.
The price they owe, naught else can pay.
Your life, in endless torment stay
If this command you not obey.
A father's blood if unavenged

Makes plagues to break, and scabs to spread
Upon the earth that festers sick
and fungus flowers as on a corpse
Unburied. . . .'"

The condition of the Mycenean state! The words shook Electra as though she too heard them from the oracle, speaking through Orestes' lips. It was the law of the gods, the law of the father's blood: He who does not avenge the untimely death of father and of king, from every altar, every home, every banquet board and ritual is barred. The blood cries out from the ground and must be obeyed. But at what price—she felt the shudder of Orestes' body pass through their tight-gripped hands into her own. For the Furies of primordial time pursued the matricide.

Orestes turned to her. In the young man's face the eyes suddenly were the bewildered ones of the boy to whom she'd bid farewell on that fateful day. *Can I put my trust in oracles like these, or not? Even though I cannot, yet must I do the deed.*

He must. She sent the thought surging back to him with all her will. He drew breath deeply. "By the grace of heaven, by my own hands' doing, *she shall pay.* I swear it on my father's bones. Do you hear me, Gods? Once her life is ended, take mine if you will; it matters not."

Oh, they were one, not just in blood and bone but in pride and passion. Electra's eyes closed on the stinging tears, and she flung her head back in the dawn wind. "Fates, hear our prayer! The voice of Justice cries. Father, from that other world, look on your children crying out our grief!"

"Father, your son calls you: stand now at my side."

"Your daughter calls, with tears that are never dried."

"Here with one voice we echo the cry you cried."

Zeus and all gods, stand with us against our enemies, and strike for Justice. Their voices like birds soaring and swooping, interwove in the morning air. A spell to Agamemnon; a spell to

Zeus. Evoking affirmation and blessing from the dead. Summoning them . . . for a moment something almost in the form of Agamemnon seemed to shimmer in the silver sky and then was gone. They were alone, they two, with only silent Pylades beside them on the mountainside. And the skies did not thunder, the walled city did not tumble, no bolt of lightning was hurled down.

It was up to them then. She had known it all along. And Orestes, too. His eyes, meeting hers, were somber.

"None from outside can help. We must, ourselves, wind up the curse and staunch the wound that bleeds our race."

The House of Atreus, House of Tantalus, of which they were the last. What must be, must be, however great the price. She shuddered again and to her astonishment felt a strong hand touch her arm. Pylades, looking at her with kindly eyes. Never, in her womanhood, had a man looked at her thus, in tenderness and compassion. In that instant, she was alive again, and a hot flush filled her with a consciousness of how she looked—gaunt, uncared for, dishevelled. In another place, another time . . . but she was burnt-out now, by the sickness of the hating years.

"What I wonder . . ." Orestes' voice, bemused, cut in across the disturbing thoughts. "Why now, so late, did *she* send libations, propitiations for a wrong no care can cure?"

"She dreamed a dream," Electra said dully. "She who never trusted irrational oracles, do you remember? But now night-walking terrors frighten her."

Orestes frowned. "Do you know what the vision was?"

Electra had heard from the old nurse. She told him.

His eyes darkened with strange fire. "This dream snake came forth from the same womb as I, its gaping mouth clutched the breast that once fed me. If it thus mingled her sweet milk with blood, then *I* must transmute my nature and become a viper. The dream commands me be her murderer."

It was as if in that moment Apollo's sign blazed before them, filling them all with iron. Orestes spoke swiftly. "Electra, you must go back. Return to the palace, disarm suspicion. Pylades and I, dressed in these foreign clothes, will come with Phocian accents to the Lion Gate—strangers seeking shelter."

"If our mother is afraid—"

"It lies with you to see that she is not. But if she is"—his mouth twisted—"we will wait. Outside the gate. And passersby will wonder that the House of Atreus is so filled up with supernatural fears. Will speculate why King Aegisthus makes the suppliants wait. . . . Once I see *him* sitting on our father's throne, once we come face to face, and he looks upon me. . . ." Orestes' hand tightened on the bronze hilt of his sword. Out of nowhere, a cold fear swept Electra. Then he relaxed, and finished simply. "He will be a dead man. Your task, my sister, is to keep watch indoors, and to make sure our old nurse keeps a prudent tongue. For yourself, speak or be silent, as each new moment asks."

Their hands met; clasped fiercely. "May Hermes follow, witness, guide and bless my sword's ordeal."

They parted, went their separate directions, and the wind whistled over the deserted grave with its lock of hair and laurel wreath.

XV · FURIES

I T WAS ALL SO easy. Day trudged by, as the city on the mountaintop waited under the white sun. Aegisthus plotted with his counselors, and the people labored under the yoke of their daily round. In her room, alone, Clytemnestra lay upon her couch, and dark visions passed before her eyes. In another chamber Electra kept apart, lest her blazing eyes and pounding heart betray her. In the olive grove beneath the hill, two figures waited. And presently Apollo's chariot began to ride lower in the heavens. The light grew greyer, faded into dark.

As Night's murky car drove from the east across the watching skies, two travelers in Phocian cloaks approached the Lion Gate. The gatekeeper was slow, unused to interruptions at that hour, so the Parnassian accents of the strangers' calls were clearly heard by idlers on the city walls.

"Hulloa! Does no one stir in Atreus' city? Is anyone in the palace? Open these doors, if Aegisthus' house is used to treating strangers well!"

A shuffling within; irritable response. "All right, I hear. What is your name, and what your city?"

"Phocians, with message for the king. We will speak directly to the guards at the palace door." And then Orestes, face shadowed by his mantle, brushed past the man, and Pylades with him, striding up the long ramp to the inner fastness.

Eight years, a lifetime, since the boy he had been had played on these very streets, teased the same doorman. They all were older now, and time had wrought changes. Orestes hesitated at the road bend, remembering just in time he must feign not to know the way. Then they were hurrying up the final ramp, along the Cyclopean wall. A few more lengths. Just a few more lengths and then, the gods willing, he would be face to face at last with his father's killers.

He did not let himself think, *face to face with my mother.*

The north stairway. Past the guardrooms, where soldiers with unfamiliar faces listened to his brief story. Then they were at the grand entrance with its two columned porticoes, and the door between was being opened grudgingly by a surly slave.

Orestes made his voice brusque, deepening his accent. "Take word to your masters that I come to deliver news. And be quick; it grows dark, time for travelers to seek refuge at a friendly inn. Ask someone in authority to come at once."

The slave stared at him with hostility but no recognition. Orestes' hand, hidden by his cloak, gripped his sword hilt. But the court, and the wide passage beyond it, were deserted. Pylades, sensing his uneasiness, touched his other arm. Then, down the corridor from the megaron, a faint sound came. The whisper of sandals on the stone. A woman's figure, its shadow distorted in the torch flames. A husky voice spoke, awakening old memories.

Clytemnestra.

Clytemnestra in a crimson cloak, all gold-embroidered, wrapped around her pleated linen. Clytemnestra like a painted effigy of her old beauty, but the same implacable eyes blazing from behind their rims of kohl.

Orestes turned away abruptly. It was Pylades who quietly, civilly, repeated what they had earlier spoken to the slave.

"Say what you have to say. This house can offer all travelers need—warm baths, a restful bed and entertainment. As for your message, speak it to me and I will report it."

This was Orestes' right. Pylades hesitated. Then Orestes' voice came, and if it was with effort his tone did not betray it. "We are Daulians, traveling with merchandise to Argos. Along the way we met a stranger, also from Phocis, Strophius by name." Once he had begun the words flowed smoothly. Oh, they of the House of Atreus were skilled deceivers; they had been taught by masters. He wished he could watch *her* boldly, to observe reactions, but he could not—for many reasons. "Since we were bound for Argos, he charged me to deliver a message faithfully. Orestes, who was prince of this house, is dead. It is for his family to decide if he should be brought home or rest in Phocis as an honored guest. The mourning rituals due to him have been observed, and his ashes lie in bronze."

Something flared briefly in Clytemnestra's eyes. Relief? Triumph? Grief? He dared not face her closely, lest his family likeness be observed.

"O irresistible curse haunting our unhappy house. Now our only hope to charm the curse away is gone."

Conventional, appropriate words, betraying nothing, and Orestes matched them. "I only wish I could have been the bringer of good news to so royal and rich a house."

"You shall enjoy no less a welcome." She turned to the slave. "Show these men indoors. Provide them baths and food and entertainment. I must report this news to the king and consult the council."

She must go to Aegisthus, and he would tell her what to do. She had never expected a time would come when she would turn to him for strength and guidance, but they were doomed to be alone together in their joint guilt. She had never expected to feel the mixture of emotions that wracked her now. A child dead. A threat removed.

She had not expected that she still could *feel*.

She must not run; hostile eyes would speculate upon the cause. She must remember that she was a queen. Aegisthus, that distorted parody of Agamemnon who had betrayed her, was the king. He was gambling with his cohorts in his private quarters, and she strode there firmly, her head high. Before her, slaves hurried to announce her coming.

In the guest quarters, Orestes and Pylades submitted to being bathed, perfumed, robed in fresh garments. Food was brought, fruit and cheese and wine. A slave girl played upon the lute. They waited.

In her own chamber, Electra paced the floor, trying to still the tumult surging in her. Orestes had come home. The time was ripe. They might fail. They must not, could not fail. The blood of the Atrean curse throbbed in her temples, and there was no relief.

A cry, a keening in the halls. Her heart almost stopped. Then the curtain of the doorway was thrust aside and old Cilissa tottered in, tears running down her cheeks.

"Oh, my lamb. Orestes our little love is dead. That lock of hair was brought here from his corpse, and now the strangers meet with the king to tell the story. How he'll hug himself with joy, that creature, when he hears it. Oh, my Orestes . . . bless his heart. I took him newborn from his mother's arms, and oh, the times he cried for me in the night. . . ."

"How does *she* bear the news?"

"Ah, there's a sad look in the eyes, put on for servants, but underneath she laughs. *She* didn't mother him."

"No, it was you. And I." Electra wrapped her arms around the old woman tightly. "Do not grieve. We have grieved for the past, and the past is ended now. Remember, 'The gods

attend to matters that concern the gods.' Put off your tears and
fetch me ceremonial garments and water that I might bathe."

The nurse's eyes widened in alarm. "You have gone mad."

"No! I think that for the first time in eighteen years I am
truly sane!"

She could see, so clearly, the god-sent visions that danced
before her eyes. Swiftly she stripped off the garments of her
shame, snapped orders for maids to brush the neglected hair.
The court clothing that she had so long avoided was clasped
round her like armor. She gazed at her reflection in the bronze
mirror, and some unrecognized recollection nagged her, but she
put it by. Her head was lifted proudly. The years of suffering
had made the bones of her face become pronounced, so that in
flickering light her visage was like a primitive mask, oddly
alluring.

I am Electra, princess, daughter of Agamemnon. The words
throbbed in her brain. How dared she have thought herself
unworthy. If her breasts were still small, a maid's breasts, they
had known no shame; it was Clytemnestra's that were filled
with poison.

She dismissed her maids, ordering them to go to their rooms
and stay there, and such was the power in her face they dared
not disobey. The nurse too, hurt and bereft, went with them.
And then she alone, in her jewels and tight basque and pleated
linen, hastened up narrow corridors, up twisting stairs, until she
stood on the highest watchpoint of the palace, where once the
Watcher had stood awaiting signs from Troy.

When she went round the corner of the monolith stone, she
could look directly down into the courtyard of the megaron.
There, like toys in the hands of gods, figures moved. A slave lit
torches along the walls. From the guest quarters a shadow
lengthened on the painted floor. A figure came, garbed in the
raiment of the royal house, that courtesy offered by it to travelers.

For an instant, Electra's eyes were dazzled. It was her father's form she saw there. Agamemnon of the same shape and stature, splendid in his manhood, about to leave for Troy. Then it was again Orestes—father; son; so very much the same.

From the portico emerged another figure, but so very different —the family resemblance distorted, dissipated. Aegisthus, with too much paint upon his raddled face, in ritual robes. Aegisthus, pretending he had come from worship, pretending grief at the terrible news from Phocis.

She could hear no words, but their gestures were enough. Orestes, acting out his role of stranger, wanderer, describing for the king the death of the kingdom's heir. Aegisthus, groping for the dignity that became his station, indicating that he was about to sacrifice to Orestes' spirit. Inviting, it would seem, the guest to join them.

The two forms moved toward the portico where the figures of the three gods stood. Electra leaned over the parapet, straining to see.

The animal brought. The garlanding. The prayers; the libations poured. Aegisthus washing his hands, offering the basin courteously to Orestes, who refused, indicating he was already cleansed. Slaves bringing the blood bowl, bringing the meal-cakes, bringing fire. Aegisthus casting the cakes upon the altar. Cutting a lock of hair from the bullock's head to place on the sacred fire. Slaughtering the beast. Inviting Orestes to do the quartering.

Orestes flinging off the handsome cloak, the tunic. His hands drawing the bronze sword from its scabbard. Now, *now*, Electra's heart pounded. But no; Orestes did as the king had bid him.

Aegisthus lifted the entrails, the sacred inward parts; gazed at them, frowning, as if he perceived an evil omen. Turned toward the altar. *Now*, the word rang urgently in Electra's temples. *Now*, the wind cried in the night sky.

Orestes lifted the sword in both his hands and brought it down, like Zeus's thunderbolt, on Aegisthus' spine.

Aegisthus' body jerked up and down, and he cried out in the agony of bloody death.

The world went black, went red before Electra's eyes. *If only I had been a man. If only I could have done it. But it was his right.* Yet I too, Electra, princess, am of the House of Atreus!

Her vision cleared. She stared down on the figure of Orestes, figure of Agamemnon, and in that moment it was as if she were one with him in body, totally united.

There were cries and shouting. Slaves rushed for their spears. Orestes, swinging round, held up his sword with a mighty cry. And the light of the torches fell upon it. Fell upon him, standing there in the splendor of his manhood, and every line of body, every feature of his face, was Agamemnon's. A murmur like the sea swept round the circle; the guards fell back, and some of them fumbled for hidden charms.

They knew, now. Orestes, last best hope of the House of Atreus, had come home.

One fled, crying, shouting, through the corridors up to the royal quarters. And then the footsteps came. High-arched, patrician footsteps in their golden sandals tapping over the painted stones.

Clytemnestra stood in the portico, back-lit by the fire blazing on the inner hearth. Over the body of the slain Aegisthus and the smoke of sacrifice, mother and son stared into each other's eyes. And a cry burst from Clytemnestra's throat. The recognition cry.

Had some god given her the gift of special hearing, Electra wondered. Suddenly she could hear everything most clearly.

"O gods, the dead have come to life. By craft we killed, by craft we die," Clytemnestra said, a dagger gleaming dully in her hand. "The long bitter story reaches its final turn."

Orestes, low-voiced, as though he dared not unleash all the words that teemed within. "It is you I seek, madam. Your lover's score is paid."

"*Madam.*" Clytemnestra's head came up. And all the old spellbinding power still was in her. "You are my son, Orestes. I am your mother. I gave you life! Let me live out my own!"

"Live—in my father's house, my father's murderer?"

"*Child!* Fate played a part; I was not all to blame."

"Then here's another death, decreed by Fate." Orestes inching forward, the bloody sword tight-clasped. The grotesque body at his feet. The stench of the entrails heavy in the altar smoke. Clytemnestra never flinching. Her hand going up to her shoulder, ripping off in one gesture the embroidered cloak. Her own hands cupping her bare breasts.

"My own child, you drew life and strength from these. Your head lay here, sleeping." Slowly, imperceptibly, she moved towards him. She was his mother; she was also the woman most beautiful in all of Hellas next to Helen. A tremor wracked Orestes' frame.

No, Electra flung at him silently with all the force of her taut being. No, she is the temptress, she is the serpent. Remember who you are and your sacred vow!

Orestes' voice shook. "You bore me; you sold my body and my throne."

"Sold! What is the price I got for you?"

Orestes flung a contemptuous glance towards dead Aegisthus. "I will not name him; I blush for your sins."

"*Your father sinned too!*" The cry from Clytemnestra's throat shook the heavens. "His pride! His Atrean pride! *He killed my daughter!*"

"And you killed king and husband and disowned another daughter and a son. To what do we owe highest love and loyalty, Mother?"

Behind its careful painting, Clytemnestra's face had blanched. "My dream . . . O gods, *you* are the snake I bore and fed!"

"And so you believe in oracles at last? How interesting, Mother, from you who scoffed at them and at the gods."

Was it something in his voice that frightened her? It held a strange note now that shook Electra. Suddenly Clytemnestra, the rigidly controlled, was pivoting on her toes. She ran like a frightened woman into the dromos, and Orestes followed.

A frenzy gripped Electra. Flinging off sandals she climbed, as she had in childhood, over the stone roof to where the round opening released the smoke that rose from the central hearth.

It was there, at that holy circle, that Clytemnestra knelt down pleading to the gods, and that Orestes slew her. He shut his eyes so that he could not see and held her by the hair and thrust his sword again and again into her neck. But Electra saw it all.

When it was over, she filled her lungs with that first deep breath of freedom, but no immortal songs sang in the heavens. She had expected triumph, exaltation; what she felt instead was a curious emptiness. She gazed down upon Orestes and upon the body of Clytemnestra, its golden skin all streaked with blood like wine. A woman's body with all the power gone.

How odd, Electra thought dizzily. This is the first time I have ever seen her. Not the queen. Not Mother. Not Agamemnon's wife. Not Aegisthus' woman. Just *a* woman. You are gone now, Mother. You will never again overlook me for Iphegenia. You will never again cause Father to forget me. You will never take him from me. Through all the years, I have had one single purpose. I put vengeance for the one I love most above all other loyalties, and I have won.

In the light of the altar fire Clytemnestra's face lost its humanness, became like a mask of bronze. The blood drummed like thunder in Electra's ears, and the images before her eyes shimmered and grew dark as truth burst upon her. *Like my own face.* Like *me. My* words now, like my mother's, crying of vengeance for the most-loved mattering more than any other ties. Fermenting through the years, in the cauldron of my soul. Until Orestes, my other half, came home. And now you are dead—my mother, my second self.

The darkness whirled and cracked and dissolved in a blaze of pain. And below, Orestes, like a weary Agamemnon, roused himself and groped for Clytemnestra's outstretched arm. Seized it, dragged her towards the door. He would have to display the bodies to the elders, prove their guilt and the righteousness of their execution. Prudence, honor, respect for the gods demanded it. She must stand beside him. It was her duty, and it was her right.

She stumbled across the roof but was able only to reach the parapet of the courtyard before her legs gave way. There she heard Orestes speak.

"Come all, and see! These two oppressed our land, murdered my father, stole my inheritance. They shared in guilt, and now they share in death."

The elders, called by frightened servants when the slaughter first began, had gathered. They rimmed the courtyard, forming an arc of stone. Out from among them Pylades came, his arms filled with purple cloth embroidered gold. The robe of treachery, woven by Clytemnestra. Orestes spread it out.

"See, this was the snare in which they trapped my father, hand and foot. A web of horror, made by my mother's hand. Let it witness for me the right and duty of this slaughter I have done."

Men looked one to another. A shudder shook Orestes. He raised one hand, heavily, to rub the sweat-damp hair back from his brow. "I am like a man who drives wild horses, not knowing where the race will end. Terror sings at my heart. But while I am in my right mind, I proclaim it was no sin to kill my mother. She was unclean, marked with my father's blood. Apollo commanded it, and I obeyed. I will go now, armed with an olive branch, as suppliant for cleansing at Apollo's holy ground."

He looked cold, naked there in the night wind, and so early old. Electra's heart ached, sending him strength she barely had. As though sensing her presence there, he stared upward, and a light of terror flared into his eyes.

"Look there! Look there! A woman in a murky cloak and hair of snakes! The avenging Fury who awaits the shedder of a mother's blood!"

The circle stirred to life. The head elder, trying to reassure. Orestes shaking him off, clutching Pylades' shoulders. "You cannot see these beings, but I see them, more and more. I must flee to Apollo. Pylades, take my sister and look after her!"

With a cry of agony, he rushed away. And no man raised hand to stop him, recognizing the sacred madness that burned within his brain. In twos and threes, in silence, they made their leave, until in the courtyard only the bleeding bodies bore witness to the ancient curse upon the house.

On the roof Electra lay, insensible, until Pylades came with gentle hands to lead her off.

ORESTES

V

XVI · DELPHI

I N THE SILVER HOUR before the dawn the Pythian priestess approached her place at the Temple of Apollo on the Delphic hillside. Here, through the smoking fissure called Earth's navel-stone, the god himself would possess her, through her lips speak words to be interpreted by Temple priests. Delphi was enchanting at this hour. Birds twittered, and a sweet pungency of thyme and flowers came from among the rocks.

It was so peaceful, so like all other mornings. She cast laurel and barley on the altar flame, made salutation and invocation of the gods. "First in my prayer I reverence Gaea, Mother Earth. Then her daughter Themis, who next ruled this oracle, and her successor Phoebe. And her great namesake Phoebus, Lord Apollo, great god of reason, healing and of light." Next she saluted with holy words Pallas Pronaia, and the prophetic nymphs of the Corycian cave; the fountains of Pleistos, Delphi's river; Poseidon, god of waters. Last of all the Supreme Fulfiller, Zeus.

The formalities were completed. She drew one deep breath, delighting in the sweetness of the air and the tranquil picture down the mountainside. Now she would go behind the sacred curtain, take her place upon the tripod seat of prophecy and inhale the sacred vapors.

She passed between the curtains, and a cry burst from her lips. "O fearful sight, appalling to describe!"

Upon the navel-stone in the wreath-hung inner shrine, a suppliant sat. A man polluted, blood still wet upon the hands that grasped a reeking sword. Yet upon his head, olive leaves were twined with the white wool of reverence.

How ORESTES had reached Delphi, he did not know, nor knew he when or how he had fashioned the laurel crown. He had run from Mycenae in the hours before that other dawn—unhindered, unaccompanied, a man accursed, reason and consciousness gone. He had managed only, as the whirling sea of chaos sucked him down, to cry out to Pylades, committing Electra to his care.

He could not feel. He could not even think. He had fled, through haunted days and nights, visions dogging his heels. How many days had passed, what roads he had traversed, were mysteries. Up through Corinth, and Eleusis, Thebes and Livadia, past the rocks of Mount Parnassus he had come. No ministering hands had fed him, yet he lived, and his mother's blood on sword and hands was uncongealed.

His mother's blood. His mother he had slaughtered.

Awake or asleep, that vision was ever with him, and the stench of blood and altar smoke, and her agonized cries. And those other images—born of that black, terrible figure he had seen on the roof in his last sane moment.

They were the Furies, those dark, primal shapes that dwell in the nether regions of the Underworld and are seen only, always, by the guilty hearts . . . black, wingless, loathsome, their vile breath a hiss, their hair like snakes, bloody rheum forever dripping from their baleful eyes. They only, and Clytemnestra's body, had he seen, through every moment of his awful journey.

They filled his sleep and slumbered round him when he woke.

It was the Pythian priestess' cry that roused him. He struggled up from nightmare, and the shapes and shadows of his private hell were still about him. Everywhere he saw the Furies, asleep on benches, on the floor, awaiting only awareness of his waking. But in the greyness, as dawn broke, a luminous glow swelled and took form.

Two forms, divinely powerful, divinely fair. Men, yet more than men, one on his either side. One wearing laurel, the other with winged sandals and a staff.

Apollo. The recognition stirred in the depths of Orestes' burdened brain. *Apollo and his brother Hermes, the messenger, have heard my prayers.*

Within his head, not so much heard as sensed, rang Apollo's words.

"I will not fail you. Near or far away, I am your constant guard and enemies' dread. For one brief hour now the Furies sleep. They will hound you yet through seas and islands, cities of the world, wherever earth is hard to wanderers' feet. But keep your courage firm, and bear your pain. At last, in Athens, where all suppliant hands embrace my sister's image, seek her help. There will I set you judges; there will I, who first did bid you take your mother's life, bring you deliverance from all your pain."

Orestes' parched lips struggled to reply. "Lord of light! Reason and justice, healing, all are yours. Your strength shall be my surety of promised help."

"Remember! Let no fear defeat your heart!" The light-formed figure shimmered; turned. *"Hermes my brother, be his guardian. Go with him through his journeys; guard him well. He is my suppliant, and I guarantee his sanctity. Let no man do him harm."*

A healing breeze, down from the Parnassian mountain, enfolded Orestes, soothing his fevered mind. But even as he felt for the first moment a sense of peace, a noxious vapor rose from the cleft of rock. A luminous darkness blotted out the sun.

Recoiling, Orestes shut his eyes against his mother's face.

"I am abused unceasingly among the dead. Despised and shamed I wander, by them all held guilty and condemned. And yet, the blow my own son struck, no voice protests!"

The voice, the so-remembered voice, rang in his brain. The Furies stirred in sleep.

"You ancient, ageless hags, whose presence god nor man nor beast can bear, was it for nothing that my hand so oft poured sober soothing draughts to you? Upon my midnight hearth, banquets have burned for you at your sacred hour. And now you sleep, my gifts spurned underfoot, while he who killed me mocks me to your shame! Listen, you powers of deep earth, and understand. In dream I, Clytemnestra, cry for justice!"

The Furies muttered restlessly, as dogs growl in sleep.

The dark form and the two golden ones that faced it waited.

"You murmur, but do not act. His friends are not like mine; they save him, while you sleep."

The murmurs rose to frenzy that no ears could hear. A dark wind swirled, battering against the firm gold light. The Furies keened.

"Son of Zeus, are you a god?
You set honesty aside;
You, the younger, ride roughshod
O'er elder powers; you've defied
Justice, for your suppliant's sake.
The matricide's accursed, and he,
Though strong oblations he may make,
Shall find no place where guilt is free."

The air throbbed. Before Orestes' haunted eyes a battle raged. The double edge of his plight smote him like a sword. Whatever he had done or not done, action or inaction, alike condemned him. Thou shalt not kill thy mother. Thou shalt not allow thy father to be killed and unavenged. And not a father only, but a king. The code of loyalty to blood, to tribe; the code of loyalty to alliances pledged, to a ruler crowned.

So had Agamemnon stood torn over his daughter's sacrifice for a wind for Troy. So had Clytemnestra; which bond was more potent, to spouse or child?

Was there no paradox that would bring peace, no coming-together of conflicting claims? *None,* cried the wind, sweeping down the Parnassian mountainside. *None . . . until, perhaps, after long journeyings, your wandering's done.*

Orestes stumbled out of the Delphic shrine, out past the stricken priestess. Into the wilderness, and the golden light in the wind went with him.

XVII · ATHENS

LONG WERE THE DAYS and years Orestes wandered. Over land, over sea, past islands only mariners knew. There was no rest, no peace, and the mark of the exiled fugitive was on him.

Ever at his heels he sensed the remorseless presence of the Furies, and the hot blood-reeking blasts blown from their vaporous womb assailed him.

"Orestes is accursed, and he
Shall find no place where guilt is free . . ."

Ever and again the words rang in his brain.

The dark images of curse and crime were ever with him. Yet other images, too, pale gold and glowing, grew ever more potent as the years went by. Apollo. Hermes. The guide of the traveler and the benign healer holding out ahead the light of peace and reason.

On he traveled, through tribes and towns where the blood-stained history of the House of Atreus was unknown, where he was recognized only as a stranger in deep suffering, needing succor. He was given succor, by people barbarous by Mycenean standards, who honored his unvoiced cry for sanctuary and gave him warmth and food.

It was in the spring when he at last made his way up over the rosy rocks to Athene's temple. The stumbling panic with which he had fled Mycenae had changed, in these long, haunted months, to the quiet rhythmic gait true travelers know.

The Furies still were at his heels. But they were no longer unknown terrors. What was it his tutor had told him, long ago? That men on battlefields become used to Death, if not as friend, nonetheless as companion most familiar.

Up and up Orestes climbed, to where the sacred temple crowned the heights above a stirring city. The air here was mountain air, making him think of home.

Home. He had never thought to recall Mycenae in that way again.

He walked between the pillars of the shrine, and the divine peace of sacred places fell softly on him. The statue of Athene, all-wise, all-knowing, gazed at him with eyes serene.

Would she listen? Or would she, like the Delphic priestess, turn in horror from the pollution of his presence?

He was a fugitive. A matricide, Orestes thought, tasting still the horror of the word. But no more unclean; he could not still be unclean! For an instant, pictures of lonely sacrifices in the wilderness, of ritual bathing in huts and palaces, flashed before his eyes. Surely, that long wandering had washed the blood off of his hands!

As those welcoming homes, the loving kindness of strangers everywhere, has rubbed the bitter hatred from my soul.

He did not know from where his words came; they were simply there. He recognized the truth of them; accepted it. He *had* changed. But was that enough?

Clytemnestra was dead, and at his hand. What was done could not be undone.

He knelt.

"Divine Athene, at Apollo's word, I come. You, who alone can truly judge, pronounce your judgment."

A faint warmth of the rising sun, filtering through the pillars, touched his face. A breeze was on his back, and in it, clearer far than human words, he heard the Furies' cry.

"A mother's blood once spilt
None can restore again;
Out of the dust it cries,
A dark, accusing stain.
. . . every mortal soul
Whose pride has once transgressed
The sanctity of guest,
God, parent pays the toll."

For how long those words had battered at his ears . . . as sentence; as a curse hurled on him from without. He heard them now, as for the first time, with new ears.

Why . . . this too was truth. Description of simple fact. Had he not, just now, thought the same thing himself?

Orestes lifted his head, looking at Athene's statue with unflinching eyes.

Would he ever be free from the guilt-haunted mirror the Furies held ever-present before his eyes?

The answers waited for him in this sacred place.

He rose.

The voice that came to his waiting ears was not Athene's but his own.

"From holy lips, with pure words, I invoke Athene to my aid. To her I compact myself, my country and its citizens in loyal, lasting, unreserved allegiance. Where'er she is, may she now come in divine authority and save my soul."

Those were not the words of a maddened fugitive. They were
. . . his brain cleared suddenly. They were the words of a he-
reditary king whose throne was yet unclaimed, making the immemorial covenant between god and country.

Into the moment of clarity the so-familiar voices of the Furies
rang. *"Neither Apollo nor Athene, reason nor wisdom, has
power to save the guilty from the Primal darkness, that consciousness of guilt in blood and bone."*

The grey mists swirled, engulfing him again. He must remember that he was no more Orestes, a second Agamemnon,
king; lost, castoff, an exile and a wanderer, he would live forever alien. Prey to bloodsucking powers. A pale ghost. The joy
of life forgot.

The chant, like the words of old ritual, drummed in his ears:

"Now, by truth's altar,
Over the victim
Ripe for our ritual,
Sing this enchantment:
A song without music,
A sword in the sense,
A song in the heart,
And a fire in the brain;
A clamour of furies
That paralyze reason,
A ringing of terror
That tolls in the soul. . . ."

Why, his heart cried out in torment. Why this conflict in
loyalties, conflict in laws given us by the gods? Why this eternal
struggle, which engulfs each generation like a curse?

The answer came, like a pattern in tapestry which had always
been there, waiting until one had the eyes to see.

The laws of the gods—the old gods of instinct or the new ones of reason—were eternal because they reflected the two sides of being human. Those laws conflicted because life was no simple thing, because we did not know ourselves or one another.

The words burst from his lips. "Are we then always doomed? Must we always break one law or loyalty to keep another? Is there no escaping, ever, from the Furies?"

Apollo's words rang in his ears. *"Go to Athene."*

The sun rose high, and with its spreading warmth a sense of harmonic stillness spread. The air danced with particles of golden light, and the music of the spheres sang in his ears. And with it, slowly, slowly, there came a pulsing, like the beating of his heart but more profound, more strong. Growing ever nearer, ever more dazzling, until awestruck, overwhelmed, he swung round and fell upon his face on the marble floor.

The goddess was coming.

He felt the presence, and the music, soaring and enfolding, as though he were caught up into a sphere of celestial light. *She* was there, the divine woman, at once the embodiment and source of wisdom, tranquility, and life. There was no more torment, no more pain. She was above him, and beyond him; she was also somehow within him, and he in her. It was as if encased in that divinity, that peace, he heard the distant, dim, familiar voices of the Furies that had so long plagued him.

> *"Daughter of Zeus, you know by sight*
> *We, the Children of the Night*
> *Who haunt the guilty, and pursue*
> *The matricide. Our judgement true*
> *None can deny. Whose hands are pure*
> *Lives untroubled and secure;*
> *But when blood is foully shed,*
> *We bear witness for the dead."*

The divine voice, compassionate yet detached, spoke graciously. *"You name this man his mother's murderer. Surely some compulsive power drove him to this dreadful deed?"*

Question answered by question: *"Who has power to goad a man to matricide? What can be stronger than the fear of such a guilt? The law lives on. We claim the price of blood."*

"You seek the form of justice, more than to be just. The letter, not the spirit, of the law."

The two voices, one gentle, one unyielding, were like the clashing of opposing music.

"Fear enforces goodness,
And it must reign enthroned
To teach through pain and sorrow
That sin is not condoned.
What man, what town, what country,
When fear is cast away,
Will bow the knee to justice,
As in an earlier day?"

And the counter melody:

"Seek neither license, where no laws compel,
Nor slavery beneath a tyrant's rods.
Where liberty and rule are balanced well,
Harmony follows as the gift of gods."

Did he see and hear with actual eyes and ears? Was this all delusion, or god-given vision? Were there, as he thought, a crowd of people suddenly gathered near—citizens of Athens, come to act as a jury of his peers?

He did not know. Perhaps he would never know. What was real was the peace suddenly flooding through him, concurrent with the Fury-fear . . . and the divine presence . . . and the trial, unrolling before him like a scroll.

He heard his own voice, telling how after years of exile he had come home to kill his mother in retribution for his father's death. Telling the promptings of Apollo's oracle, and more, the sense he had had of Apollo's presence with him, Apollo's hand on his as he performed the deed.

Just as he had it now. The light in the temple grew more golden, glowing. Orestes' heart swelled. *Apollo was here.* Apollo has come, to speak as his intercessor, as he had promised.

The Furies, as the accusers, were speaking first, and he bravely answered.

"Did you kill your mother?"

"With a sword I pierced her."

"On whose persuasion?"

"That of my own instincts, and of Apollo, whose reason showed my mother twice guilty, twice condemned."

"How so?"

"She killed her husband, and she killed my father."

"The man she killed was not of her own blood. You killed the source of your blood, of your own life."

"My father was the source of my life, too!"

"Your mother killed the killer of her child!"

Statement unanswerable. Dilemma as intertwined as the Gordian knot. Orestes cried out: "Apollo, tell me! Was I right to kill her? Is murder justified?"

Reason spoke for Orestes through Apollo's lips. Instinct responded in the Furies' cry. Higher and higher the arguments piled, each so just, so irrefutable, building up on either side. Like the weapons of opposing armies. Like casualties upon a battlefield.

Like white and black pebbles cast by jurors into blindfold Justice's scale.

Equal balance.

Silence shimmered in the stillness like breath caught and held. Orestes, his whole body hurting with the pain of the long waiting.

The Furies, their cry now silenced, waiting.

Apollo, waiting.

Retribution? Absolution?

Only Athene, goddess of wisdom, could decide.

The voice came softly, the voice of divine Wisdom speaking with infinite grace. Casting the deciding vote—a white pebble. Forgiveness; absolution. Siding with reason, for when instinct and logic are equally opposed, reason must govern; for who can ever be wholly sure our instinctive acts spring from the blessed gods and not from the furies in our souls?

The clamor had stilled. A caressing warmth touched Orestes through the dazzling mist that filled his eyes, and he turned toward it. Beyond the temple pillars lay the long way up which he had come. Athene's city, silver and pearl, and beyond it mountains and plains and sea.

He *knew*, now . . . Athene's verdict, and so much more. From what he had run, and why, and why it had been folly. Not folly because there could be no escape, but because there was no need. He had feared death—not an end to being, but the dark terrors of the final judgement; all the horror conjured by that vision of Clytemnestra at Delphi, long ago . . . *abused unceasingly among the dead, despised and shamed, by all held guilty and condemned.* He had run shrieking from that fate, not trusting in Apollo's pledge he would not die. Not trusting Apollo's will, or power, to save his life—not realizing Apollo's words had been no promise of triumph in future conflict, but plain fact.

He had not died, because his death was immaterial—the Furies had consumed him while he was yet alive. The festering, guilty human heart was the cave from whence they sprang.

Reason could not defeat them. Only Athene's gift of wisdom,

born of suffering, could transform them into Kindly Ones—joined hand in hand with logic to protect one from rash actions sprung from the dangerous recesses of the unknown self.

Dazzled, Orestes turned and, in humility and gratitude, flung himself face downward on the marble floor.

The sun blazed brighter, a white heat. How long he lay there, he never knew. When at last he rose, strength had returned. Exile and wanderer no more, no more an alien, he was confirmed as king and as a man. The air was rich with the scents of a hundred flowers, and the sky was very blue, and serene in the shimmering distance the blue sea beckoned, calling him home to the palace on the mountaintop above the Lion Gate. The Furies, like lions, had roared themselves to silence and had been transformed into Eumenides, the Kindly Ones, the voice of conscience that protects and prospers all who give reverence with clear, unfearing eyes.

The sense of divine presences, at once so warming and so threatening to man, was fading. There remained a faint thread of music and a sense of peace. Orestes took a deep breath, looking westward toward where the sea was dancing in the sun. For an instant another vision, born of both instinct and reason, dazzled before his eyes. A vision of a land where blessings breathed in wind and sunlight, where beasts and fields, well-treated, enriched the people with unwearying fruitfulness. Where sons and daughters guarded the fair peace, sternly uprooting rank weeds of impiousness under the guidance of the Eumenides. These were the blessings he must bring about, he and his people; they could be wrought only out of one's own inner tranquility. They could not be bought by blood or begged from the gods.

Mycenae, he thought. The throne is waiting. Electra and Pylades. A whole lifetime.

It was time to go home.

Orestes plucked a sprig of thyme from between the rocks before Athene's temple and tucked it carefully into his girdle.

He picked up his traveler's cloak and wrapped it round him and began to walk, slowly and then faster, down the steps of stone. He was not even conscious that he was whistling.

The curse on the House of Atreus was at an end.